White Roses

A Memoir

Holding The Impossible:
A love story before and after death

Janis A. Pryor

WHITE ROSES – A MEMOIR

Copyright 2017 – Janis A. Pryor

Printed in the United States of America

Names, places and other identifying details have been changed to protect and respect the privacy of individuals involved. Two characters are composites, and the timing of some events have been compressed in the interest of storytelling.

ISBN – 978-0-692-14026-0

Published by Black Pawn Press

FIRST EDITION

This book is dedicated to all of those whose truth is stranger than fiction and to J.S., who knows this truth.

... white roses speak of a love that is eternal,

a love stronger than death, all sustaining,

with unchanging loyalty ...

The Request...

On the morning of May 5, 2013, looking at that panoramic view of Mt. Washington from the living room, I felt two hands on my shoulders, and then heard a voice I recognized. *"Tell our story. Tell what was and what was meant to be. Do what I read you could do and finish it by the end of May."* It was the voice of the man I knew I was going to marry, Tony Carter. He died in 2007.

Part One

Before

"...tell what was..."

CHAPTER ONE

May 5, 2013

Before The Man With The Wonderful Hair

What happened to me on May 5, 2013 and the subsequent experiences didn't come out of nowhere. Being genetically predisposed to see the dead, I was the fourth generation to have this and related abilities. According to family lore, it started with my maternal great grandfather, my grandmother's father and trickled down.

My ability to do this was verified at the age of three. I woke up one early winter morning and saw my Uncle George seated on the foot of my bed, glowing in this soft, yellow light. We had a conversation that didn't become clear for decades until I was ready to hear it. Uncle George had died from tuberculosis, long before I was born when he was twenty-one.

I remember running into the kitchen and telling my grandparents while struggling to climb and seat myself in a kitchen chair while saying, "Mama, Mama, I just saw Uncle George. He was sitting on my bed."

This was just another piece of information as far as my grandparents were concerned. They weren't shocked or alarmed. There were no admonishments, no denial. It was just information like the weather, the time of day or the day of the week.

My grandmother said something like, "You did? Okay." She continued fixing breakfast while my grandfather nodded his head in acknowledgement. Neither one of them said I was crazy nor making it up.

The second experience happened roughly two years later when I was five. There was a fire on the narrow street behind our house. Such commotion from the perspective of a five year old was overwhelming. There were fire trucks, sirens, people screaming. My grandfather and I stood in the kitchen door and watched one of the houses burn down to its foundation. I looked up at the night sky right over the house and saw three figures, two adults and a child rising up.

"Papa, Papa, look," I said pointing to the sky. "Are those people going to heaven?"

"I hope so, Pumpkin. I hope so," he said. The next day in the newspaper there was a story about the fire. Three people had died, two adults and a child.

My grandparents, who raised me, understood that their only grandchild would straddle the world of spirit and the western world grounded in science and/or fact. One of the first questions I remember asking my grandfather had to do with God, the Creator, the Great Mystery. Understanding and knowing God or the Great Mystery was important to me even as a child. I spent time pondering what many couldn't see or feel. No one knew this except my grandparents. I was seeing that other world through the veil, often, and developing an array of different ways of knowing.

Raised in two radically different parts of the United States, the Gulf Coast of Mississippi and New York City's Manhattan island, with the blood of three races running through my veins (The Mississippi Band of the Choctaw Nation, African-American and white European) I often came across as an oddity or a puzzle to black and white people. I defied too many stereotypes. As one of my white acquaintances said, "You're a citizen of the world!" One thing was very clear to me, early in my New York City school life, not everybody could see the dead, and those that could were often perceived as strange, sick or crazy. I kept my mouth shut.

I come from a highly educated, complex family with no simple answers regarding who they were or how they achieved their status and material security in the deepest part of the south, the Gulf Coast of Mississippi. They had enough status, security and know-how to buy a brownstone on the Upper (North) West Side of Manhattan during the 1950s. It was a community predominantly populated by survivors of the Holocaust and their children. This was no small thing for an African American family to achieve at that time.

My bicoastal life was fueled by education. It was *the priority* in my household. There were three generations of college graduates in my family. I had to "get smart!" Getting smart required spending the school year in New York City with summers on the Gulf Coast and later, Bennington College. One result? I loved thinking and pondering the improbable. So I devoured books and became a keen observer of people. The result? Early I.Q. tests classified me as "highly gifted." And that led to being "tracked" or placed in special advancement classes for the intellectually gifted. I glided through grade one to grade twelve. New York City fed my intellect and talents for art and the theatre that couldn't be had any place else.

The other result? I became a fashion monster able to find Armani in any store like a heat seeking missile! My mother, Tina, was obsessed with my appearance because when I grew up, black women were considered ugly, unattractive, promiscuous and obese. And given that my mother was very fair (or light-skinned) my skin color represented an additional problem. Depending on my hair, people might mistake me for Latina, Philippine or Native American, but not white.

My mother saw me as a threat and was frightened of me. I was smart in ways she didn't understand, and I never conformed to her idea of what her daughter should be. Most of all, there was this "psychic thing" and that terrified her. Writing this book forced me to find out everything I could about this psychic thing I had that showed itself in another way when I first met my mother at age five. I remember looking in her eyes that day. I didn't know exactly what was wrong with her but I did know "she had too many people in her." As time went on, it was impossible to predict which one of her personalities would pop out. She was a superb actress and was what Jewish philosopher, Martin Buber, described as "malignantly narcissistic." M. Scott Peck's book, *People of The Lie, The Hope for Healing Human Evil,* cites the psychoanalyst, humanistic philosopher, Erich Fromm, referring to his broadened definition of necrophilia. This broadened definition includes "the desire of certain people to control others – to make them controllable, to foster their dependency, to discourage their capacity to think for themselves. To diminish their unpredictability and originality, to keep them in line." This is a form of evil according to M. Scott Peck, *anything* that seeks to kill life or liveliness, *that seeks to murder the body or the spirit*. This was my mother. She fought me and won many battles but lost the war. To understand how I became who I am one must know something about her because what's "normal" for me is a lot different from everybody else.

After May 5, 2013, I spent a lot of time recalling things I had heard from my great-aunts, my grandmother, and general "gossip" among my grandparents' friends about people like me, people who had this different way of knowing, who heard things no one else around them heard, and saw what they described as "beyond the veil." Until now, this was my little secret. On May 5, 2013 I was forced to pay attention and driven to understand what this was all about since it presented itself in such a dramatic fashion. The definition of who I am was incomplete. I had to face the fact that although I was a quiet person, I wasn't living a quiet life.

Imagine being able to sense a person's true intent, to read between the lines, and see beyond the masks we all wear as we go about our daily lives? I walk into a room full of people and often get all kinds of information about the nature of what struggles people were going through. It's worse than seeing them naked! Sometimes it's like looking at the landscape of their soul. Too often in my personal life and occasionally in my professional life I ignored or dismissed information received this way and paid for it!

My grandfather, Papa, died in 1980. Mama died in 1989. I went "home" to Gulfport, for the funeral. Walking into the living room the power of my grandparents' presence stopped me, and I said out loud, "Oh my God, they're here." Experiencing their presence felt like running into an invisible force field. That night, sleeping in my childhood bedroom, I felt the edge of the bed sink. Turning over I saw my grandmother sitting there while my grandfather sat in a nearby chair, smoking his pipe. The comfort was enormous. The gratitude for being able to see them was beyond articulation.

Since their transition, my experiences and different ways of knowing expanded. They became subtle but powerful companions advising and protecting me, professionally and personally, in unexpected ways. I could never put this on a resume however.

Now roughly thirty-five years after their deaths, I knew my grandparents had prepared me for what happened on the morning of May 5, 2013. Looking at that panoramic view of Mt. Washington from the living room, I felt two hands on my shoulders, and then heard a voice I recognized. *"Tell our story. Tell what was and what was meant to be. Do what I read you could do and finish it by the end of May.*" It was the voice of the man I knew I was going to marry, Tony Carter. He died in 2007.

On May 28, 2013, twenty-three days later, the first draft of what you're about to read was finished. I still don't know why he wanted me to finish it by the end of the month unless he considered May, "his month." He was born in May. I ended up writing most of *White Roses* in the middle of the night between 11 PM and 2:30 AM in my bedroom. There were no distractions then.

Three or four days into writing that draft a small image of a well known actor appeared in the corner of my bedroom. He plays the lead role in a popular television series. I remember laughing and thinking I had been watching way too much television. Within days that image filled the entire room. I stopped writing. Something was up. This was not my imagination.

I looked at the image of the actor. He did not look like Tony. Leaning back in bed, I heard Tony's voice. "This is my emissary. He will help you through some difficult times while writing this. You'll find me in his eyes. There's a teacher coming to help also. She has a comical connection to the emissary." And then Tony was gone. I didn't understand the connection. But I knew enough to know, something was up. At that moment, I didn't realize I had already made an unconscious connection with the Emissary.

I started researching this emissary. Social media can be a wonderful resource. I looked at every photo I could find of him and discovered three shots that made me stop breathing. The shock of the energy coming through the emissary's eyes was the exact spirit of Tony. Both had a distinctive physicality. Both were at ease with their bodies. They shared a fondness for the same color and went to the same college but each for only two years. They shared a passion for issues, activism and politics and came from complicated families. There were other similarities they shared but I knew I was still missing something. I found the emissary's biography, and there it was in the very last line. They shared the same birthday.

The emissary did get me through some difficult times while writing this in very unexpected, amusing, and comforting ways. I found the teacher just a few miles from where I live – and yes – she had a comical connection to him. At least, it made me laugh when I met her.

Revealing all of this is hard because I am a very private person. But the need to start having intelligent conversations about impossible things transcends my comfort.

CHAPTER TWO

Who Is This Man?

Spring 2005

Like most days when I was in New York City and not at my country place in the Hudson River Valley, the end of the day was signified by walking my American Cocker Spaniels, Spike and Yoko Ono, around 5:30 or 6 PM. I adored them. I stood at the corner and watched cars fly down West End Avenue. I noticed the days were getting longer, the air a little warmer.

The light changed and we walked down the street to Riverside. As I turned the corner I saw my close friend, Christine, slowly walking towards her building. She saw me and waved. I waved back and caught up to her. She was holding a tote bag with books packed in to the straining point. I could see the leather seams beginning to give. Christine was a big woman, not heavy or fat, just big boned, tall and formidable looking. She had flawless brown skin and jet black hair tightly braided into an intricate pattern. She was brilliant, a college professor who taught Contemporary Political Science at Columbia University. Two children and a husband, who was an attorney, filled out her domestic profile.

"Hey," Christine said. "What's going on?" and she sat the tote down on the sidewalk.

"Listen," I said. "I've been meaning to ask you something."

Christine patted Yoko and Spike. Standing up, she looked at me and said, "Ask away."

I pointed to a metallic navy blue, late model BMW parked across from her building. "Do you know who owns this BMW?"

"How would I know?" Christine managed to frown and smile at the same time.

"Well, he probably lives somewhere right here, maybe in your building. How many people could there be? I've seen him for years drive a series of BMWs. You know I love those cars. Remember how I drove one for ten years?"

Christine stared at me. "Yeah, I remember. You drove it into the ground! Let me get this straight. You want me to go looking for a strange man in New York City who might be living where? In my building?"

"He's not strange! He's right here somewhere. You do know him. I know that."

"Hmph. Okay… What is this? A gut feeling on your part? Your gut feelings can scare the shit out of me sometimes."

"Stop. Just go look for him," I urged.

"Why can't you find out?" Christine asked me.

"I'm not doing that! C'mon!" Seeking out information about some man for no other reason than curiosity was somehow beneath me. "I'm not going to do it," I repeated.

"But I can do that? I can go snooping around. What am I supposed to do, stake out the car?" Christine asked.

"If need be," I said.

Christine groaned and sighed. "Okay...so what does he look like? Details, girl, details! You're an artist."

Great, I thought. She's going to do it! "Okay, well...he's got wonderful hair! I like the way it's graying. There's something very appealing about it. And I guess he's about six feet. Maybe a little taller and lean, fit, very fit."

"So you're telling me he's not fat."

"No fat men in my life," I said and felt badly about saying that, but not that badly.

"Okay, I'll see what I can find out. You owe me for this," Christine said and picked up her tote bag.

I responded with, "Only if you find out who he is."

"You're too much. Let's go."

We continued to walk. I was quietly thrilled with the prospect of getting some information on this man. I had been curious for a long time.

CHAPTER THREE

The Man With The Wonderful Hair

My days ended with walking Spike and Yoko and they began with walking them also. The next morning I stumbled out of bed and managed to get us all out by 7 AM or so. With the spaniels pulling me across the street I heard, "I've been watching you for over twenty years. You don't change. The dogs don't change."

I thought I was hallucinating but I heard it again and turned around. Thankfully, I was wearing sunglasses. I could feel my eyes widen. I was stunned. It was him, the man with the wonderful hair. A wave of joy washed over me. For a minute I couldn't find my voice.

Holding several newspapers, he walked by me with a smile. I think he had on a pair of navy blue Bermuda shorts, a light blue tee-shirt, a baseball cap and some brown boating shoes. He was attractive in a very masculine way.

I realized I had to say something before he walked away. "Wait a minute. Who are you? What's your name?"

Still smiling, he looked at me and said, "Tony," and kept walking. He walked down to Riverside Drive, turned the corner and disappeared. I was immobile with shock when I realized the spaniels and I were still standing in the intersection. I stepped up on the sidewalk and knew I had to come up with ways to bump into him again. As I walked with the spaniels down to the park, something made me realize that I had just flipped a switch and it made me nervous and giddy. I would never admit that...yet. Spike and Yoko stopped to sniff some bushes and two thoughts collided in my head. *He's been watching me for twenty years? What is that? And where has he been watching me from?*

CHAPTER FOUR

Reflections

I spent more time than I wanted thinking about the what? Synchronicity? Coincidences? I asked Christine to find out who he was and the very next morning he told me. Had I talked him up? I had this feeling that somebody or something in another realm was giggling right now. Yoko Ono walked over to me and wagged her tail slowly. Spike was lying on the couch next to me and lifted his head when he saw Yoko. I looked at both of them and said, "I know it's time. It's past time." It was almost 6 PM. "Maybe we'll see Tony," I said to them. The look on their faces shouted, "We don't care. Let's go!" And that's what we did.

We had almost finished our route. I could see Christine's building and realized that I hadn't told her about the man with the wonderful hair. I knew I had to call her but right now I was enjoying the annual birth of spring. The air had that specific fragrance that told me summer was coming to New York City.

I gazed out at the Hudson River for a moment. The George Washington Bridge was not far away from where I was living now, nor from where I was born at Columbia Presbyterian Hospital, Harkness Pavilion. It overlooked the West Side Highway and the Hudson River. The brownstone my grandparents bought was on the upper west side also. The truth was I hated living in New York City but it was my base. I needed to be in New York City because so much of what I needed professionally and culturally was there, but I didn't want to be there.

I had no memory of leaving the city with my grandmother at seven weeks old. Tina, my mother, was busy pursuing a career and had no time to take care of a child, much less an infant. Her field? Early childhood education.

My first home (and the only place I considered home) was roughly ten blocks north from the white sands of the Gulf Coast, also known as the Southern Riviera or the Red Neck Riviera depending on your politics. We couldn't go to the beach because it was segregated. But there was no law against driving by and looking at it and we did. Palm trees, sand, boats, blue water, open skies, constituted my first impression of the world. Even though the South was segregated and dangerous, I always felt safe in my grandparent's home. It was one of the bigger houses compared to those of other black people down home who lived in what was called "the quarters." This was a phrase shortened by time and law from the original moniker, which was "the slave quarters."

I first remember coming to New York City when I was five years old. I was horrified by how big and crowded this city was but in awe of the grandiosity of Pennsylvania Station. My grandparents bought a four story brownstone in Manhattan. Tina, her husband, my father, Harry, my grandmother and I lived there. My grandfather joined us there full time roughly three years later. It was a move initiated by Harry's attempts to kill us in a drunken rage that came every weekend. I didn't like the brownstone.

All of us moved to Riverdale when I started attending the High School of Music & Art. I wasn't crazy about Riverdale either, although there were more trees, yards, and some cobblestone streets. It didn't matter where we lived. New York City had a way of wearing me down. The pace and the size of it toughened you. You had to be alert and watchful all the time. The masses of people generated so much information that I often wanted to scream. I escaped when I was accepted at Bennington College in Vermont. I could breathe there. There was open space, gentle green mountains and less traffic. When I arrived at Bennington the student population was three hundred. It was a relief.

I reluctantly returned to New York City after graduation because it made sense given my interests, the arts, politics and media. I was getting better at handling information I sensed from other people. I could never completely shut it down, but I understood that I wasn't obligated to move on every piece of information I picked up about people. I also began to better control my visible reactions. And, at the time my grandparents were still alive living in Riverdale. Once they passed I couldn't shake the feeling that something wanted me out of Manhattan, out of the city permanently. Eventually I did leave.

However, as a child and teen-ager, the Big Apple was responsible for opening my eyes to the breadth and depth of art, theatre, music and ballet. I started attending art school when I was 13 and I studied drama for five years. I auditioned for an off Broadway repertory company for young people when I was in high school and was accepted. I remember getting the lead for the production of Antigone. I loved MoMA and the Guggenheim. An exhibit of Nicolas de Stael at the Guggenheim changed my life. It changed the way I saw the world, the way I perceived color and form.

The issue of color is tantamount in the black community. The color caste was alive and well publically and privately, especially with my mother. My grandfather's family, being part Choctaw and part white European looked like the color wheel. Knowing this it made perfect sense that I gravitated to color field painting where color was the subject. One of the most powerful statements I was influenced by came from one of my high school painting teachers when we went to MoMA. There was an exhibit of Jackson Pollock's work. My teacher said, "Jackson Pollock freed line from configuration to carry color." That moment for me was like understanding Einstein's theory of relativity!

Broadway, the West Village, the museum mile, Fifth and Madison Avenues, the West Side Highway, Henry Hudson Parkway, anything on the west side and in Manhattan, including Zabar's, was my New York City. But it was wearing thin. New York City exacts a high price from its residents, energetically, monetarily, physically, emotionally and spiritually.

Walking back to my building with Spike and Yoko leading me, I knew it was time for me to leave Manhattan at least for a short time. I had bought some land and built a house in the country with some of the money from my inheritance. I needed to spend some time there.

I had to figure out what to do with the rest of my life given my mother's scandal that ended my political career. I always knew she was "not well." I just had no idea of the breadth and depth of her madness until I received a call from the Bronx Office of the District Attorney. Their detective informed me that she had forged my signature on some insurance documents. They knew it was a forgery because they had already checked my signature card(s). When it was all said and done, she was charged with over two hundred counts ranging from forgery to unfair labor practices. If you work for any major politician who had national prominence or had aspirations to work in the White House, you can't be news. *You* can't be a bigger story than your boss – for any reason. This had a disastrous impact on my life. It made my head hurt just thinking about it.

Deep in thought about all the lives she wrecked, I looked up and saw Tony. He was opening his car door. He saw me and smiled. I smiled and waved. We held each other's gaze for a second too long. I felt my stomach go cold and my breathing became shallow. That inner voice that resided somewhere in my head, heart, and soul pushed every thought out of my mind and told me, "You're going to marry that man." I was horrified and wanted to run!

That was absurd. I was an only child, and had lived alone for all of my adult life. I had a college roommate for *one semester*. It was much easier living with cocker spaniels! The thought of marrying some man seemed absurd. Had it not been for my grandfather and my internist, Dr. S. Kirkland, who became the closest thing I had for a father it would've been very easy for me to write off men without a second thought. Christine was always saying that I blew men off like dust on furniture! Who needed the aggravation? Anyway, *I am not qualified for a relationship. I don't do relationships.* I don't even know this man. For all I knew he could be a crazy person! Or as another friend of mine speculated sometime later, an axe murderer!

Watching the spaniels as they walked, we quickly reached the corner. What the hell was wrong with me? This man, this Tony person, really had no interest in me. He was just being polite and charming. He had only said a hand full of words. We waved at each other. That's all it was.

Lost in these concerns waiting for the light to change, the sound of a honking horn made me jump a little. I turned and saw Tony. I looked at him and he looked at me. Something clicked on some hidden level and calm washed over me. Whatever was in motion, I knew it was too late to stop it. It was out of my hands. I smiled as he drove by and he smiled back. I looked down at Spike and Yoko and said, "Let's go."

CHAPTER FIVE

The Coincidences Begin

Later that evening I went to a dinner party given by some friends who lived in the West Village. While riding down there, I really hoped they hadn't invited someone they wanted to fix me up with hoping I would fade into the blissful sunset of marriage. Last time I saw them they expressed their concern about me being alone. What I should be doing is putting some things together to take to the country, I thought. I needed to go to Zabar's, stock up on bagels, get some of their coffee just to have even though I didn't drink it, and of course, get the Nova, the best lox in New York!

I paid the cab driver and walked up the front steps of their brownstone. Richard and Daniele were good people. I really liked them. These were people who always tried to do the right thing. They often fell short and hid behind their liberal credentials, but didn't we all at one time or another? I just wanted them to calm down about marrying me off. Hopefully, we could have an animated conversation about politics or art with the other couple they invited, George and Esme and this other man they told me about.

Dinner started promptly at 8 PM. Daniele made roasted lamb. Richard was pouring wine for everyone except me. The only alcohol I could drink without getting a violent headache was Lillet Blonde. Daniele always had it on hand. The way the dining table was set made me happy and peaceful. It was a beautiful display of food, china, flatware and crystal. All of it was highlighted by candlelight. This was marred somewhat by George who already had one drink too many. This other man they invited, was Ralph Walters, an English Literature professor at NYU. He had a pudgy face and sausage like fingers. He seemed harmless and boring, harboring a lot of pain from too many rejections. Too needy. I wanted nothing to do with him.

This dinner party had a purpose. Richard tapped a spoon against a wine glass, looked at me, and announced that Daniele and he had purchased a boat with George and Esme, something called a Sabre. Photos were passed to Ralph and me. I knew nothing about boats but I knew this must have cost a ton of money. All their kids were grown, why not? Why not enjoy the money?

"Janis," George yelled!

I passed the photos along to Ralph. His pudgy face was ripe with expectation. I turned from him and said, "Yeah George. What's up?"

"I want you to come out sailing with us." He leaned back in his chair and grinned.

I sighed and said, "I don't swim. Boats frighten me. I never really understood how they stay afloat. I love the ocean but I also love the feel of land under my feet."

"No, no. I'll teach you to swim," he said. Esme gave him a severe stare.

"George, I really don't think so. I tried learning how to swim as a child. It didn't work. They say I'm a tilter." I reached for the napkin and spread it in my lap. George was seated directly opposite of me. He had loosened his tie and was revving up.

"Look, look. Let me tell you something," George said as he now leaned forward toward me. I saw Esme close her eyes and shake her head a few times. I felt her dark brown curly hair screaming at George. "You're not going to be able to get away from boats. I'll cure you of your boat phobia." George pointed his finger at me and stated, *"Boats are in your future. Boats are going to be all around you. You wait and see. Better come out with us."*

I just looked at him and said, "Okay George. If you say so." He was a hefty looking guy, the kind whose clothes never quite fit. I was just waiting for him to pop a button on his shirt the next time he laughed.

George gave me a definite nod and drank some more wine. The food was really exquisite, the conversation entertaining and informative, but I left as soon as I could without offending Daniele and Richard.

I got up earlier than usual the next morning. My intent was to go to Zabar's when it opened. Spike, Yoko and I had to get out of town. The city was suffocating me. As the three of us were walking, I saw Tony drive past me. We waved to each other and I kept walking. I heard him put on the brakes. I turned around and he was driving back down the street. What in the world was this man doing? As soon as he got to me, he stopped and lowered the passenger side window.

He leaned over and said, "I have to tell you this. I don't know why, but I do."

"Okay," I said. I was a little suspicious but also curious.

"I sail a lot. I have a boat. I've been sailing a long time. I just thought you should know." The window slid up, and he drove away.

I had been studying his face when I realized what he said. I stared at the back of his car and thought I really needed to find out more about this man. This much I already sensed; he had a good heart, he was kind and could be trusted. He was intelligent and had a sense of humor. I sensed that from his expressive eyes that seemed to dance. Not bad. I bet he would know about Sabre boats or yachts. I had to remember to ask him if he would only stand still for more than five minutes!

Spike and Yoko continued pulling me back home. As soon as I got settled, I flopped down on the couch and called Kae. She was my grandmother's niece who lived in North Carolina and one of the few living relatives I had. We started phoning each other after my grandmother died. Kae and I now talked daily, sometimes twice a day. She became very much like my grandmother and what Tina should have been. You have to hold on to people who stand up for you, and Kae did. Kae's daughter was also named Janice, spelled with i c e versus Janis, i s. When we talked one of us became Jan and the other simply, "gurl."

"Kae, I've got to tell you about this man. It's the strangest thing." I explained how I talked him up and was running into him now when I'd rarely seen him before. I told Kae about his car and boat. "I don't even know who he is."

Kae was silent for a moment. I could feel something coming. "You better go make friends with this man, Janis."

"Make friends with? I don't even know him. The whole thing is just plain strange."

"You better listen to me and go make friends with Sailor Man," Kae said in a very firm tone. "This is the one."

"Oh Kae!" She was confirming what I sensed and I hated the significance of that.

We talked for an hour about everything from the weather to the Bible, but we both knew Sailor Man was cruising just beneath the surface of our conversation and we both knew that he was the one.

I sat wondering what I could do to reach Tony. I got up, walked into my office and found a pad of paper. I sat down and wrote, "Where do you sail?" I wrote down my email address, folded the paper in thirds, sealed it with some tape and my cocker-spaniel stamp. During our last walk around 9:30 PM, I placed the note under his windshield and affixed it with another piece of tape. Hopefully it wouldn't blow away.

The next morning, standing at the end of his block I saw Tony open the note. He looked around first. I stood frozen with my two impatient spaniels watching him. Tony opened and read my note, and then I saw him smile. It was like watching the morning sunrise. He folded the note, put it in his pocket and drove off.

Later that day I received an email from him. "What a pleasant surprise! I usually sail out on the island, the Hamptons, Montauk, over to the Connecticut side of the Sound. Sometimes up the Hudson."

I made sure I ran into him that evening. By now I had an idea of his arrivals and departures. I saw him park his car and waved. The spaniels and I walked quickly to meet him. I didn't bother saying hello. "Have you ever sailed up the coast of Maine?"

"No. I've sailed in the Caribbean." I thought he looked amused or happy. His face did light up.

"Well, you should. The coast of Maine is amazing," I said.

He locked his car and stepped up on the sidewalk. Spike and Yoko pulled me over to him. They sniffed Tony out and their tails wagged with abandon. They liked him. My God, I thought. I looked up at him and for the first time got a visceral understanding of how tall he was. "Have you ever been to Greece?"

He just stood there, smiled and said, "No."

"You should go. Go to Santorini. See it before you die. It is one of my favorite places on the planet."

"So you've been?" he asked and leaned back on his car.

"Yes. It's gorgeous. You should go, charter a boat and sail to a few islands. Just make sure one of them is Santorini." I bent down to pull off a leaf that had become part of Yoko's ear. I could feel Tony watching me as I stood up. "Some friends of mine have bought a boat, a Sabre yacht."

His eyebrows raised and he said, "Wow. That's some serious money. It wouldn't be my choice..."

We gazed at each other looking for something neither one of us wanted to identify nor admit to yet. He sighed, smiled and said, "Did I just sound like a jerk?"

"Oh no," I said. "Not at all. You're entitled to your opinion." I could barely think at that moment.

"You know," he said, "I'm not an American citizen."

"Really? Where are you from?" I noticed he wasn't wearing anything blue!

"Jamaica. We came here when I was nine years old."

"So you're familiar with the Caribbean. That's why you were sailing there."

Still smiling he said, "Yeah, I had a friend who wanted me to take off a few months and sail with him from here down to Bermuda one year. But that wasn't in my plan."

I smiled while thinking, my God! A man with a plan. I felt like I was in a trance.

"I have to go," he said.

"Oh, okay. You take good care."

He leaned forward, smiled at me and walked across the street. That's when I realized he lived in Christine's building. He had probably been watching me from his condo. I just stood there trying to comprehend this. Opening the door for Tony, the doorman waved at me. I'd known him for years. He knew every spaniel I'd owned. I waved back and continued our walk. I felt like my head was going to explode. Who is Tony?! I had to talk to Kae and I really had to get out of the city.

Days later, I was still in Manhattan and had not gotten to Zabar's, but I had received several emails from Tony and that evening I saw him. He was getting into his car and the spaniels, as usual, were pulling me down the street. I caught Tony's eye and he nodded in recognition. As I got to his car and stopped, he lowered the window on the passenger side. I leaned down and asked, "What do you do?"

"I work with artificial intelligence," he said. "Some of it is classified."

"Oh...that's interesting, intense." The only thing I knew about computers was that I hated them and artificial intelligence made me fear for the future. The possibility of computers becoming smarter than we are was too real.

"I make good money," he said and grinned. "So what does your husband do?"

The question jolted me. "I don't have one," I said. I thought he looked pleased.

"You work?" he asked with some doubt in his voice. He had such kind, caring eyes.

"Yeah. I work." What is he trying to figure out, I wondered?

"*Really?*" Now he sounded surprised.

"Really! What's so odd about that?"

"Absolutely nothing," he declared and smiled. "I gotta go," he said and drove away. He had a great smile that said more than what he was vocalizing.

This was some fancy flirting. Wait until I talked to Kae! But Sailor Man would have to wait. I had to get out of the city. Head up to the Valley and paint. Art, painting, drawing, designing, these were the only things that completely occupied my mind. It pushed aside everything else. There was no room for any other thoughts. I could focus. No room for this Tony person.

I had to figure out how to earn some money. In addition to the two hundred counts filed against her, Tina had made some very bad financial decisions before she died in December of 1999. During that last week in 1999, I told myself that the Lord was not going to let her damage another century! I was right.

Her objective was always to control me. She told me if I returned to Riverdale and lived with her she would let me have the rest of my inheritance from my grandparents. I refused to do that. As a result, I lost huge amounts of cash. I was the beneficiary on several life insurance policies from my grandparents that I never saw. Accounts vanished. Property my grandfather left me was sold without my knowledge or consent until after the fact. That's where her fondness for forgery came in handy. Right after my grandmother died I told her I was going to court. Suddenly she agreed to mediation. There were two years that were too painful to ever talk about. She never completely let go of my money.

Shortly after Harry died, Tina took that opportunity to tell me that he left me nothing because I was a "bad daughter." Considering that he tried to kill me on at least one occasion and tried to kill Mama, I didn't care. I barely knew the man. We never had one exchange that could remotely be called a conversation. Papa, Harry, and I would eat dinner in virtual silence while Mama and Tina watched us eat from the kitchen. Fighting off Tina's toxicity was a full time job. There was no energy to even think about Harry! The thought of telling Tony about *any* of this made me want to cry. What would he think about me?

Right now, I had just enough money to live without working a traditional job. I had to find something to supplement the inheritance that had been reduced by Tina and her bad judgment that left no cushion for the country's economic disaster caused by the housing crisis.

My grandparents decided I had to come north to go to school. We all lived there in the brownstone they purchased. Tina was a graduate of Spelman College with a Master's Degree from Columbia University. That's how she got to New York. She was very smart, but she was also a functional alcoholic. She married

Harry, my father, who wasn't much better. He was a binge alcoholic. The weekends were hell. The closest thing to a conversation he and I ever had took place when I had to hospitalize Tina.

For some reason he couldn't call an ambulance nor her doctor. I received a call from the housekeeper begging me to come and "do something" because Tina was "very sick, something was very wrong." It was my birthday. I drove up to Riverdale disgusted and depressed. Was this ever going to end? Dr. Kirkland was on vacation and I didn't know who Tina's doctor was. It took the housekeeper and me almost forty minutes to get Tina in my car. I told her I was going to call an ambulance if she didn't let us take her to the hospital.

The housekeeper and I returned from admitting Tina to the hospital, two hours later. She was diagnosed with one of the worst cases of alcohol poisoning the emergency room doctor had ever seen! I walked into the living room and Harry asked me, "Where is she?" I told him, "In the hospital. Montefiore," And that was it. It was a stressful situation, the end of which I had already seen. Thank God for my grandparents.

A little over ten years later, her madness was revealed to the world. My vindication and validation finally arrived when I received that call from the Bronx Office of the District Attorney. It was a nightmare the full extent to which I never understood until she died. Tina kept insisting that it would "blow over." It didn't. How would I tell Tony? How? I was haunted by these questions.

He'd go running and screaming down the street. I knew I would eventually have to tell him.

A few days later I was finally ready to head up to the Hudson Valley and escape. All I had to do was go to Zabar's. Just as I was leaving, the phone rang. I almost didn't answer it but something told me to pick it up. It was Kae and she sounded upset.

"What's wrong?" I asked.

"I want you to go on your computer and find out just who this man is that my Janice is marrying."

Frowning, I asked, "What's going on?"

"I think he's a criminal," Kae said. "I don't know where she found him. He doesn't work...just layin' up on her all day." Mae was in her seventies and not to be toyed with.

"Well, I don't know what I can do. I'm no computer wiz. I'm lucky I can turn the thing on!"

"Janis, something's wrong with this man. Do you hear me?"

"I hear you. I'll do what I can, but you need to tell me this man's name. Do you have a social security number?"

"No."

"Okay. Give me his full name and where he was born."

"Get a pencil and everything. I wish you could see him. He's out there in the yard now..." Kae mumbled. "Did you get your pencil?"

"I got it."

Kae cleared her throat. "All right, He was born in Gainesville, Florida in 1972. His name is Anthony Carter. See what you can find out."

"Okay. I'm trying to get up to the house later today. I'll call you when I get there and get settled this evening. Maybe I'll have found out something or at least have some ideas."

"Good. But I'm telling you that man's a criminal!"

Poor Anthony Carter, I thought. God help him.

Zabar's was crowded. I always tried to get there in the morning but it was after noon now. I was usually as faithful as the tock after the tick. There was a clerk I always went to, Wally. Thankfully he was still there. He saw me and motioned me over to a less crowded area. I gave him my list.

"You must be going up to your country place," Wally said while reviewing the list. "Stay right there, Janis. I'll take care of this for you."

While waiting for my order I wondered what this Anthony Carter had done to get on Kae's bad side. Laziness was a bad way to start a relationship with Kae. Crossing Kae was just plain stupid. Wally returned with my order neatly packed in a Zabar's bag. I gave him my credit card.

"How's your mother doing Wally?"

"Much better. Thanks for asking? You going up to do some painting?" he asked and handed me my order.

"I am. You take good care." I put on my sunglasses.

"I will," Wally said and smiled.

I picked up the shopping bag, turned around and walked right into this man's chest! I apologized and looked up. It was Tony. He was dressed in jeans and a dark blue tweed sport's jacket. I tried not to look too excited.

Before I could say anything, he said, "I was just getting some things. You like this place?"

"Yes, and you?" I started to walk out.

"Yeah. Hold on. I'll walk you out," and he gently touched my elbow. Once we were outside, he looked at me and said, "Must be nice – to write and paint pictures all day."

I had never told him anything about my art and I hadn't published anything in over a decade. Maybe he overheard me talking to Wally. It unnerved me and then I remembered the internet, search engines, and Google.

"Listen, it's not a hobby. It's my work. You seem to know all about me, but I don't even know who you are. Just Tony, who does something with artificial intelligence, lives on Riverside Drive, waves really well, and drives a BMW! That's not much."

"What do you want to know?" He looked like he was trying not to laugh.

"What's your full name? We could start there," I said.

"Carter, Tony Carter."

I took off my sunglasses and stared at him.

"What's wrong?" he asked.

"Your name is Anthony Carter?"

"That's my name. What's wrong?"

"I... I just had a conversation with a relative whose daughter is...married to someone also named Anthony Carter." I didn't want to tell him Kae's daughter was also named Janice.

"Maybe he's a relative," Tony said. "I have a large family." He smiled. "You never know."

This tall, good looking man with the wonderful hair, dancing eyes and an amazing face; the kind of face you wanted to sculpt; an appearance that made one of my white friends think he was white with eyes that spoke a different language than his mouth was compelling. He was doing something that frightened me, but I didn't care. He was edging his way into my heart.

The interior of his car was always pristine. He dressed well. And as my grandmother would've said, "He's got a good paying job." A job that I knew was more than it appeared to be, that had some element of danger. I felt it twice when we were talking.

What would Kae say now about Sailor Man? One thing I definitely knew. There were too many damned coincidences. Something or someone had to give.

CHAPTER SIX

Disclosures

With the spaniels in the back seat we drove up the West Side Highway to the Henry Hudson Parkway and then onto the Taconic Parkway. It took me an hour and a half to get to my house if I obeyed the speed limit and traffic was moving. If I didn't obey the limit, I could often get there in an hour. On this day, I split the difference and arrived in an hour and fifteen minutes.

The country house was my personal creation. It was two acres of green, open space with a spectacular view of open fields and low rolling hills. I wanted it to embody the specifics of my life and my needs, warmth, comfort and beauty. I did believe you should not have anything in your house that was not either useful or beautiful. I wanted people to feel like they were hugged when they walked in. My house felt lush, inviting and contemporary, but not severe. One of my favorite pieces of furniture was the Charles Eames lounge chair.

I wanted people to walk in and touch things, the thick wool throws in the living room, ceramic bowls and mugs, beautifully woven baskets. I wanted guests to look at paintings, sculptures, posters, photographs, framed architectural renderings. I wanted them to take books from the shelves, thumb through them with care and discover new worlds, images and ideas. Books populated the house like ants at a picnic. I played music constantly everything from the top forty to Celtic music to soundtracks from theatre productions and the movies. Plants were everywhere, breathing, growing and keeping the spaniels and me company.

Windows allowed light to pour in like liquid gold. The bedrooms were full of quilts, fluffy comforters, and down pillows. There was a spot designated for a life sized, silver blue-gray sculpture of a woman who exuded the energy and appearance of a Priestess done by an artist I discovered at Paradise City Arts Festival. Rooms often smelled of cedar, sage and roses all in memory to my grandfather who had a way with roses. At night, the house looked like it was lit by fireflies surrounded by two open acres that in turn were framed by wooded areas. Hawks often flew overhead and frequently landed near the house. They had special meaning to me and I wondered if I would ever have the chance to tell Tony.

As I pulled into the driveway I saw Lucinda's car. She was my housekeeper and my protector! She was small in stature maybe five feet tall, with short black hair, dark eyes and tan skin. She's what some kids call "fierce." Looking at her made me think of that quote from Shakespeare, "And though she be little, she is fierce." Intimidating was another word that fit Lucinda like a tailored suit and she wore it well. Spike and Yoko had already run through the short breezeway from the garage to the back door. They barked two or three times. By the time I got to the door, Lucinda had already opened it.

"Oh, Miss Janis, you have some bags from Zabar's?"

"I do," I said and hugged her. "It's good to see you."

"You been away too long," Lucinda said as she reached into the back seat of my car and took the bag from Zabar's. "You just tell me when you want me to come down to the city."

We walked down the back hall into the kitchen and dining area. "Lucinda, I need to talk to you. There's this man," I said.

"Oh," she said and her voice jumped an octave. She started unpacking the bag from Zabar's and putting things away while I took off the spaniels' leashes. "Before I forget, your cousin, Miss Kae, called just a few minutes ago."

I filled Spike and Yoko's water bowls with fresh water first. "Okay, I'll call her back. I know what she wants. But sit. I'll fix some tea for us," I said.

"No, no, no! You let me do that," Lucinda said.

I looked at her, pointed to the dining table and said, "Sit. I've got this."

Frowning, Lucinda sat, and I told her about the man with the wonderful hair and all the coincidences. Lucinda was silent for a few seconds after I finished and I placed a cup of tea in front of her. She picked it up, took a few sips and then looked straight at me. "You really like this man."

"I don't know enough about him to really like him. He won't stand still long..."

"Miss Janis, stop. I don't know what's going on here but I know it's something strange. Too many coincidences. Somebody wants you two to know each other. Okay, so here are my concerns. One, what the hell was he doing watching you for twenty years? I don't know about that. Okay? Now two..." and she drank some more tea before she continued. "Nobody," said Lucinda, "*nobody* going to do to you what that other fool did. Nobody!" She slammed the spoon down on the table. "That man was no good for you. He take advantage of you. He was jealous. You very smart. I know all that you do. I been with you for a long time. That fool wasn't as smart as you. I get so mad when I think about all that you did for him, how you *helped him get ahead*. That first piece you helped him write that was printed! My God. That wouldn't have happened without you. The opportunities he grabbed for himself and never thought about you and then didn't know how to handle them. All those famous people... He never been anywhere before he met you! Oh my God, he makes me sick just thinking about him."

I sat mesmerized. I never heard Lucinda talk about this chapter in my life with, "The Fool," as everyone who knew called him. Kae couldn't stand him either and went so far as to call him once and gave him a piece of her mind. Maybe Kae and Lucinda had talked at some point.

Lucinda not only had a fierce attitude, she was loyal and tough. Growing up in Nicaragua under the Sandinistas did that. There was more to Lucinda than what you thought. She left college to become a member of the Sandinistas. Her work made her a target for the right wing. The Sandinistas hustled her out of the country to save her life. I always believed that one day she would return.

Lucinda got up with her cup of tea, walked over to the kitchen counter, turned and looked at me before continuing. Yoko then jumped up in Lucinda's chair. Spike had gone into the living room and leaped up on the couch.

"Miss Janis, I never understood why he did what he did. He just kicked you to the curb to go off and marry some plain little woman with bad taste and simple needs. And he had the nerve to invite you to the wedding! He's a crazy person! And then he called you while on his honeymoon! It was months before you were okay. Almost a year. Nobody knows how bad it was except me. So listen, if this new person, what's his name?"

"Tony. Tony Carter."

"Okay, if Tony Carter do any harm to you, *it will be bad for him*. I'll kill him with my bare hands. Nobody understands how much you've done for people over the years. I do. I been watching. I know what you've done just for me. So, if I meet Tony Carter, I'm going to let him know. Okay." Lucinda walked over to me, sighed and asked, "What you want for dinner?"

Dinner? Who needs dinner? I wanted to talk to Tony Carter. I wanted to tell him about all of this stuff, the coincidences, my family, my life, how he struck me, what I knew about him, and I have to tell him that I see dead people too and had different ways of knowing things. (The Fool wanted no parts of that piece of my reality. It spooked him.) I wanted to know why Tony walked funny. It was a distinctive walk, but funny. He walked like he wasn't used to having legs! It probably had something to do with sailing. A friend said, maybe it was a case of sea legs. But there was a certain athletic swag to his walk also that told you he was in full command of his body. Wait until Kae heard about all of this. There wasn't too much that was important that Kae didn't know about me.

I spent several days at the house, painting and thinking, in that order. Spike, Yoko and I took long, quiet walks. I did discover some information about the other Anthony Carter. He did have a record! Sometime during adolescence something bad happened, but his records were sealed. That's all Kae needed to feel confident about her impressions. I could hear her now. "Janis, sometimes I can just feel things."

I called Christine. I hadn't talked to her in some time. I finally told her about Tony Carter.

"Tony," she exclaimed! "I know him. He's been around forever! So what's going on?"

"I don't know but I will. I've got to tell him about all these 'encounters'. Something's …funny." I left it at that and asked about her kids and her husband. She ignored my inquiries.

"Are you going to tell him about that nine-eleven incident?" she asked.

"Christine! It's bad enough you know. Oh for God's sake! I hadn't planned on it." We squabbled for a few minutes before hanging up. The incident she was referring to happened a week to the day before nine-eleven. I was talking on the phone to a friend in Boston whose husband was going to Los Angeles the following week. We weren't close friends. We talked maybe two or three times a year and saw each other even less.

I told her to tell him not to go. The sentence just rolled out of my mouth, the same way you'd ask someone to pass the bread. She wanted to know why. I said, "Because he'll die." I remember the silence that followed.

"How do you know this Janis?" Her voice became chilled and distant.

"I don't know. I just do. Do whatever you want but I'm telling you he's going to die. He should take another flight, or postpone it all together."

She slammed the phone down and I never heard from her again. The following Tuesday was nine-eleven, and we know what happened to that Los Angeles flight departing from Boston. I don't know if her husband lived or died.

The minute I got back to the city, I emailed Tony and listed all of the coincidences. I hit the send button a little after 1 PM. I knew he'd be getting home later today. I can't explain how I knew. I just did. I waited a half hour later to walk Spike and Yoko that evening. I was glad the days were growing longer. It was mid-May. The air was full of hope and pregnant with possibilities.

I spent a few minutes talking to the doorman for Tony and Christine's building. We chatted about the cost of living in New York City and how absurd it was becoming. I walked across the street and leaned against the stone fence that overlooked the Hudson River, the West Side Highway and bordered the park. I waited, nervous and a little terrified. What was this man going to think? Fifteen or twenty minutes later, I saw Tony park his car and get out. He locked it, looked up to the side, and saw me. This studied smile evolved as he slowly walked towards me.

As he approached, he said, "What were those words you used to describe what was going on between the two of us?"

"Serendipity, synchronicity. I thought you needed to know." I was so scared that he was going to walk away, making it clear that he never wanted to see me again.

Standing not more than a foot and a half in front of me, he said, "I believe in all that you know." He loosened his tie and unbuttoned his shirt collar.

"Really? You're not just saying that?" I asked. I wanted to weep and dance for joy. Maybe there's hope.

"No. I believe in fate, destiny, serendipity, all of it. So when I read your email..." he said, smiled and stepped closer. "I'm *glad* you told me. I'm glad you *could* tell me. Wow."

I closed my eyes for a second and sighed. Looking up at him I said, "So, you think maybe we're supposed to know each other?"

He paused and scanned my face before saying, "...or something," He bent down to play with the spaniels. Standing back up he looked at me for another second or two.

Somebody drove by with their radio blaring an Alicia Keys' song. I heard, "Everything's going to be all right, all right..." Still inches from me, I could sense his physical strength. I could feel the heat flying from his body. And I could feel him thinking. I felt the hesitation and the range of questions going through his mind along with his insecurities. It was a dramatically visceral sensation. I wondered how many people could feel or sense something like this. If only I knew someone else who was like me. Meanwhile, my heart felt like it was going to explode.

"I've gotta go," he said. Then he turned to walk across the street and I snapped.

"You know something, you've *always* got to go. I think you're scared of me, Tony Carter. That's what I think. I don't get it. I really don't." I saw him stop and bite his lower lip, but I didn't care. I didn't care what he did. He could go play in traffic! I turned away and said to Spike and Yoko, "C'mon, let's go." The next thing happened so quickly and so smoothly, it seemed like time stopped. I felt his hand on my arm and I turned around to look at him ready to give him a piece of my mind. Watching me for twenty years! What *is* that? Then there was this whisper of a kiss.

He stepped back a little, smiled at me and said, "*Hi...I really do have to go.*"

I didn't know what to do. I didn't know why he said, hi. I wondered if it really happened at all but the look on his face and the way I was feeling said something happened and would continue to happen. It would just be different.

"I have to go see my sister tonight. Just remember, fate, destiny...I believe in all that. You know, your ears are turning red." He smiled and walked across the street to his building.

I stood there and watched him until he went inside. The doorman waved to me. I think I smiled, waved back and walked home.

CHAPTER SEVEN

Sidewalk Romance

We fell into a routine of meeting at the beginning and end of the day. We'd meet on the sidewalk and talk sometimes for only a minute or two, sometimes longer. The weather often prevented our meeting, but rarely a sighting of each other if we were in the city. I'd vanish for stretches when I went to the country and he would go on vacation. These meetings were the highlights of my day. I'd report faithfully to Kae. She was delighted but she couldn't figure out why this man was taking so long to simply ask me out. I choose not to dwell on that. Something was brewing. I just wasn't sure what. All I knew was it was going to be life changing.

There were conversations that were turning points for us, in the sense of getting to know each other. Very early one morning, I was walking up his block with Spike and Yoko. I saw him leave his building and walk towards me. The way he was looking at me made my eyes widen with worry. I heard myself say, "Now what?"

Spike and Yoko were wagging their tails. Yoko was pulling me towards Tony so she could jump up on him. He finally stood right in front of me and said, "You are so intelligent and articulate." But the tone made me feel like he was seducing me!

"Where did that come from?" I asked. I pulled Yoko back and softly said to her, "Sit." Spike was busy sniffing Tony's shoes.

When Spike finished, he sat down in front of Tony, looked up at him and wagged his little tail with approval.

"I heard you on the radio over the weekend," Tony said.

"Oh…that." I muttered. "I thought I told you about that."

"No, you didn't," he said.

"Well, I had to find a way to make some extra money and this came along. I auditioned and got the job."

"You really engage the audience. It was interesting, informative." He slowly looked me up and down. His eyes finally rested on my face.

"I can't even remember what the subject was. They're taped in advance," I said feeling self-conscious.

"You read a lot, don't you?"

Another woman walked by with her chocolate lab and said, "Hi Janis!" She was a regular dog walker just like I was. Her greeting broke the sexual tension that was going to explode if she hadn't come along. I knew my face was beginning to turn red. I could feel the heat.

I nodded my head towards her and said, "Hi," wondering where Tony was going with this line of inquiry. I wasn't sure how much more I could take. Collapsing would not be a good thing to do right now.

"When do you find the time?" he asked. "You do so much."

One thing I had learned about Tony was that he was insatiably curious. He could be so charming that you never felt he was being nosy.

I looked at him and managed to say, "I don't date."

He just stood there looking at me, eyes wide with incredulity, and said, "What?"

I repeated myself and added, "I don't date. I don't have time."

His mouth fell slightly open for a second and then he glanced down at his watch. Looking back up at me, I knew he was trying to compose himself and had a thousand questions.

Before he could say anything, I announced, "I know. You've got to go! See ya' later," and started to walk back to my place with the spaniels.

"We're not finished with this," he said with a raised voice. "What about brothers and sisters?"

Still walking, I yelled back, "Nope. No siblings, no husband, no parents, no aunts and uncles, no first cousins." I turned briefly to look at him and said, "Just me and the spaniels." I kept walking and grinned from ear to ear as the three of us finished our morning walk.

He kept his word. A few days later he found me sitting on a bench in the dog park while watching Spike and Yoko play. He sat so close to me the sides of our bodies were almost touching. Tony leaned forward, turned his head to face me and said, "You're alone."

I wasn't expecting that. He caught me unprepared. "Well, I guess."

"What I mean, is you don't have any family," Tony said staring at me trying to comprehend my reality. I guess it was hard if you came from a big family.

"Yeah... just distant cousins, the sons of one my grandfather's nephews."

"Where are they?"

"South, down south..." I said.

He was looking at my face as if it were a map of some sort. We just sat there. I didn't know what else to say. It never occurred to me to ask him about his family, especially his sister. She had to be important to him. He mentioned her enough in his emails that let me know she was an important part of his life. It seemed like he spent a fair amount of time with her. If he didn't say something soon I was going to start screaming!

"So, who was he?" he asked. I could barely hear him.

Confused, I said, "Who was who?"

"The one that hurt you so badly." He wasn't smiling and looked almost somber, his eyes heavy with concern.

I could feel him trying to get a good look at my heart. "What are you talking about?" I asked. The heart he was trying to look at was looking for a place to hide.

He sat up, leaned back and gave me a look that said, "C'mon..." and raised his eyebrows. He had one of the most expressive faces I had ever seen. It was perfect for sculpting.

Exasperated, I sighed, faced him and said, "There's no need to go into it. *It is long over.*"

Tony bent his head down slightly, looked at me again with those eyes that repeated, "C'mon. What happened?"

With some hesitation, I looked him in the eye before speaking. "Okay. Imagine this. Imagine me being a wine glass. He took it, threw it on the floor and stomped on it. Now you know, at least from my perspective. I don't know what he would say."

Tony was speechless. He started to say something but stopped.

"Now you know what he did to me. Like I said, that was a long time ago. It's really over but I'll never forget it." It felt like hours passed before he said anything.

"What?! Was he crazy?" Tony asked.

"No, he was scared," I said. "I represented too much of a risk for him. Too many conventions would be broken, and he was a very conventional, traditional man who worried about pleasing people all the time."

"Where is he now?"

"I don't know. Somewhere. I don't follow his movements," I said. "I haven't seen him in several years."

"He was a coward. That's what he was. And he left you? He's insane. I would never leave you."

I could tell by the look on his face that Tony was mad and perplexed. I wanted him to drop the subject but he didn't. Some long seconds passed before he said anything.

"*What* world is this you come from?" he asked, eyes almost twinkling now.

"I don't know. But he'd never seen it, I guess. He led a sheltered life. Hadn't seen much. Had barely travelled. He'd never been outside of the United States, and hated the beach! He was smart. Just didn't know as much as he thought he did. Had a healthy dose of rigidity."

"Where ever your world is I want to be part of it," Tony said.

Then it was me who stood up and said, "I've got to go." I called Spike and Yoko and we headed home, leaving Tony seated on the bench thinking. As we walked home, that voice in my head asked, "Did you hear what he said? He would never leave you."

Once home, I fed the spaniels and thought that maybe all of "this" was too hard as I turned on the radio. This, being this thing that was going on with "this Tony person." I was confused and distraught to the extent that I was dizzy but also delighted. I liked Tony Carter. I could admit that now. *This was a man I wanted in my life.* Standing behind my couch I focused on the radio. Playing again was that song, "Everything's going to be all right, all right."

"What's going to be all right?" I almost yelled. Spike stared at me for a moment. "And *when* is it going to be all right? When!!"

The phone rang and I discovered Christine on the other end.

"Hey, what's going on?" I asked and tried to compose myself.

"Listen, I thought you should know," Christine said. I could tell she was chewing something.

"Know what?" My voice was barely a controlled whisper.

"Your tall, handsome friend, Tony Carter, also known as Anthony Jacob Ian Carter the third, has been asking questions about you.

I could just feel her beaming on the other end. I climbed over the back of the couch and flopped down. "Really?" I asked while motioning for Spike and Yoko to join me.

"So, what is going on between you two?" she asked.

"Never mind that. How do you know he was asking questions about me?"

"Because he asked me," Christine said.

I groaned. "Tell me what he asked."

"He wanted to know about your background. He thinks you're rich," Christine said.

"Did you straighten that out? Am I going to have to track him down now and correct whatever propaganda you told him?" I looked around my living room, and surveyed the clothes I was wearing, wondering if he'd ever seen me drive. If so, I could understand why he might think that. SAABs weren't cheap cars but that didn't mean I was rich. That was a simplistic assumption. My dramatic relationship with money was not easy to explain. Half the time I didn't understand it. The absence of money was never a problem in my family. It was the presence of it and in what form; who controlled it, how much power it gave you, and what to do with it. I knew exactly how much my life cost them. Tina made sure I never forgot what I "cost" her, what my monetary worth was. She took out a life insurance policy on me. And she wondered why I started having migraines at the age of nine. She was the only one who was mystified.

"What's to straighten out? You think he's looking at your clothes, your car? Got nothing to do with that. I keep trying to tell you this."

"Well then, what the hell is it?" I demanded.

"It's *you*. How you carry yourself, how you talk, what you know, who you know! You've got this air about you. That's what he's curious about. C'mon Janis. You walk in *a lotta different* worlds all the time. You are comfortable just about everywhere. That's what he's reacting to. That's what everybody reacts to. Remember that dinner we went to over on the East Side? It was some political event. I'm standing around trying to look like I knew what I was doing, trying not to break anything, hoping my Ph. D in political science would cover my insecurities, and what were you doing? Having some in-depth conversation with the former Secretary of Labor! You knew about the art work these people had... my God. What's normal and common to you is mind blowing for the rest of us!"

"If you say so," I said and paused. "Have you ever really listened to the sound of his voice?

"Janis...what are you talking about?"

"The *sound* of his voice is very unusual. How would you describe it?" I asked.

Christine was silent for several seconds. "Well, I never thought about it. Look, I'm not listening to his voice the way you listen to it. I'm a married woman with children."

"I could be blind and I'd know that voice," I said.

"Okay...what's with the voice now?"

"It's sort of hollow but it can be soothing. It can be enticing. It's just different.... It's a full voice...but..."

"You're losing me. Do I need to come over there?" Christine asked.

"Look, let me call you later." I hung up and ate dinner. The sound of his voice started playing in my head. I didn't know why but I knew it was important that I remember the sound of his voice. I found it distinctive.

I called Kae. I had talked to her earlier about some news story but I needed to talk to her again.

"Kae, it's me," I said.

"Are you okay? You know I had some dreams about you and Sailor Man."

"Kae... I barely know the man. We haven't spent all that much time together. It's just some casual encounters on the sidewalk. It is unlike anything I ever..."

She cut me off and said, "Don't you let this man get away from you!" This phrase was becoming her mantra.

I sighed and responded with, "Kae, please... it's just strange." We talked for at least a half hour, more politics, more weather, more reflections on faith and spirituality, the usual.

I used to meditate on a regular basis and stopped. Tonight I decided would be a good time to resume. I didn't know what happened when other people meditated. I went places, saw things, heard things and was given information. From time to time I would draw what I had seen and occasionally make notes.

Back in the eighties I drew scenes from the first past life recall I had. For months and months after that every Friday night at 9 PM these automatic drawings would push their way through my fingers. I was not above tracking down a good psychic and seeing them from time to time when I couldn't figure something out, or was just plain befuddled. Right now Tony Carter was the source of my befuddlement. But I didn't need a psychic to tell me what *my* problem was. I said to myself, "Don't fall for this man. Don't do it!" And then there was this other voice. "It's too late! This is meant to be, regardless."

I turned on the television. I had worked in television as an editorial director, producer and coordinating producer for a documentary that garnered two major awards before doing some freelance work. One of those projects ended up airing on the BBC. People who worked in television either watched it all the time or never watched it unless somebody put a gun to their head! Regardless, I was an informed viewer. Television also became a source of white noise when I was reading or painting, and/or a prophetic medium for me. It was one way I determined what issues had surfaced in the mainstream or what situations would behoove me to seriously consider especially given my work in politics. It was rare for me to have the television off.

Meditation would not embrace the white noise of television. I needed silence. With Spike and Yoko next to me I settled in and remembered an earlier conversation with Tony that I found both shocking and comforting.

He had opened the trunk of his car and it was spotless! The only thing visible was a beautiful tennis racket and a few yellow tennis balls.

"Oh," I said surprised. "You play tennis?"

"Yeah, trying to fight off old age," he stated with a grin. "Why? Do you play?"

"I used to and I played badly," I admitted. "But I love the sport. It's the only sport I can really watch and enjoy. How do you find time to play tennis and sail?" I didn't really care. I just wanted to keep him talking!

He closed the trunk of his car and said, "In the summer it's easy. I'll go to church on Wednesday evenings and sail or play tennis on the weekends."

"You go to church?" I asked with serious interest.

"Oh yeah. The first thing my mother did when we arrived in this country was find an Episcopal church for us to attend, and I've been going there ever since." He paused for less than a second and then said with a sneaky smile, "I pray for my wicked soul."

"I don't think it's so wicked," I said. "Where do you go?"

We stood there smiling at each other for a few seconds and I thought, "This is so ridiculous!"

He told me the name of his church and I was a little stunned. It was a beautiful, well known church. I always walked by and never stepped inside. The church had such a sense of gravitas and historical significance that I couldn't imagine any ordinary human being actually worshiping there. Then I realized Tony was still talking to me.

"It's a great place. They have all kinds of programs and welcome gays and lesbians."

"You're kidding," I said!

"No."

"Wow," I mumbled. "That's some fresh air."

He got in his car and said, "You should come."

I watched him drive away and reviewed my relationship with organized religion. It wasn't good. Papa detested the hypocrisy found too often in the church. I could not understand how the Bible was conveniently twisted to justify so many things that I considered "sinful:" the church's resistance to seeing women as equals, their fear of the Gnostic Gospels, their inability to accept the totality of Christ and our relationship as humans to him, and his to us as, not only an ascended being but human as well. I was convinced that the Bible was full of secrets most people were afraid of discovering. But church did offer community and that was no small thing in a world that was growing more comfortable connecting with machines than living beings. At this rate, I was afraid people would actually forget how to talk to one another unless a computer was involved.

Watching television later that evening, I thought my grandmother would be so delighted with Tony. My grandfather? Probably. Papa would take his time seeing what this man was about. Tina would adore Tony for all the wrong reasons, specifically he was "light, bright and damned near white!" Kae was already sold on him, and she'd never seen him, didn't know or care what he did. The chance of finding a decent man with a good paying job who also went to church was like hitting the trifecta. I laughed out loud.

CHAPTER EIGHT

Reflections

The spaniels and I had gone up to the country. Tony Carter was taking up too much space in my mind. He either had to get in or get out. These sidewalk flirtations and encounters were driving me crazy. Any sane woman would walk away, but I didn't. Sanity left the room a long time ago.

Lucinda was bustling around in the kitchen. The spaniels flew in and startled her but she recovered. Her face glowed as they jumped up and wagged their tails.

I loved kitchens. The kitchen, for me, was the heart *beat* of anyone's home. The living room was the intellect, the office the mind, the bedroom the soul, and in my house the studio was the heart. The hallways were like blood vessels carrying life back and forth and all throughout.

I often found resurrection outside in wide, open spaces. The land fed me. It made me feel whole and strong while the ocean was a source of enormous comfort. To look outside and see nothing but trees, sky, and mountains at any time of the year delivered peace and one with all that is, was and will be.

I walked out on the deck and stood there breathing, taking it all in. Birds were flying overhead and I recognized a hawk landing less than twenty feet from me. He spread his wings out for a moment and then folded them while looking directly at me. I smiled and nodded in recognition. Very quietly, I said, "Hello, my brother. What are you trying to tell me today?"

Decades ago, I had visited a woman who helped me discover my totem. I had already been aware of the prevalence of hawks in my life. They seemed to be everywhere I went. I found that uncanny especially when I was in the city, any city! She told me to keep alert when hawk shows up, that there is a message coming. Apparently those who attracted "hawk medicine" have visionary powers and lead you to your life purpose. Those with hawk medicine, because of their intensified life-force, must be careful how they express themselves, according to the late Ted Andrews, author of *Animal-Speak, The Spiritual & Magical Powers of Creatures Great & Small.* "These people have the ability to tear off the heads of any snakes in your life, or anyone or anything seen as an enemy. Your comments and actions will be like the hawk's beak and talons – strong and powerful, but with a capability to tear and/or kill." I learned this about myself when I was growing up. Tina proved to be my enemy countless times with her sneers, insults, denials and saccharine pretenses. The only defense I had against her was language, the spoken and written word. I watched her cut down people with a glance. Me? I had a talent for destroying people without ever laying a hand on them. This "thing" of being able to see people emotionally naked included sensing their weaknesses and conflicts. I did with words what my mother did with a glance. I could be a verbal terrorist. It was a skill I valued, and used cautiously and rarely as an adult.

Additional research revealed that "hawk people see the overall view and they should be aware of signals in their life. Hawk medicine teaches you to be observant." They see way down the road long before others. And, "many hawks mate for life."

She looked at the animal cards I had pulled in addition to hawk: deer, turkey, dolphin, buffalo, badger, ant, and skunk. I winced when I saw the skunk card and she admonished me. "Skunk," she said, "is about respect." I remembered a line in *Medicine Cards*, by Jamie Sams and David Carson that made me think of the recent conversation Christine had with me about how I carry myself. Sams and Carson state, "The carriage of your body relates to others what you believe about yourself. Skunk medicine people have the ability to attract others, and they are very charismatic. At the same time, the other side of their natural power is to repel those who seek to take energy from them without recycling the gifts they have taken." The late Ted Andrews wrote, "It is a very powerful totem with mystical and magical associations. It teaches how to give respect, expect respect, and demand respect. It helps you to recognize your own qualities and to assert them."

As I was reviewing all this in my head, brother hawk was still there, spreading his wings, turning around, and then stopping to look at me. In an instant, he shot up into the air so quickly it frightened me. It seemed almost unnatural.

I went inside. Yoko and Spike had found their respective places on the couch. Lucinda walked in and said, "You need to know something." She was wiping her hands on a dish towel.

"What's up?" I asked.

"There's been an owl flying around here," Lucinda said.

"Okay. Is there a problem with this owl?" I asked.

"I'm just telling you. This owl flies in on the deck and just sits there like he owns this place! I thought they only come out at night."

"No – day and night Lucinda," I said quietly.

"Owls and then those hawks. It's making me nervous," she said and walked back in the kitchen.

It was making me nervous too but I didn't want to tell her. Lucinda would over react, become breathless, and have to sit a few minutes to calm herself. Too often owls were omens of death and evil as well as wisdom. I had always been attracted to owls and fascinated by the fact that they could fly silently. The owl according to my two sources is a symbol of protection. "Owl can see that which others cannot, which is the essence of true wisdom," Sams and Carson say. For those with owl medicine, "no one can deceive you about what they are doing, no matter how they try..." The vision and hearing abilities of the owl have metaphysical links to the gifts of clairvoyance and clairaudience as well. Owl medicine gives you the ability to see into the darkness of others' souls and their lives. I was certainly able to see into the darkness of my mother's soul but what I knew about "The

Fool," the last man I was involved with, I ignored until circumstances forced me to confront an ugly reality about him. There were a few people I encountered who were not at all what they appeared to be much less what they wanted me to think about them. What about Tony? What did I sense? The answers to those questions started presenting themselves later that evening.

Lucinda and I talked for a bit before she went home and then I walked Spike and Yoko. With coyotes nearby I never let them off the leash. Summer was just about here. The green of budding trees and grass was fresh and clean. The rolling hills off in the distance seemed to be throbbing and preening with vegetation. The best thing about being here was the silence, the quiet punctuated by the sounds of birds or the rustling of trees when a gentle breeze drifted by. I wanted Tony to see and experience this, to witness nature's magic on the land. I had a feeling he would enjoy it just like I knew he would be left speechless by the blue and white beauty of Santorini. I daydreamed about walking on the beach with him and watching him sail. There was a heavy, thick sensation that came with those daydreams. Something else that made me uneasy. It was as if I was moving in slow motion or was walking underwater while thinking about this.

Later that night, I decided I would meditate before going to bed. Spike and Yoko understood what I was about to do. They jumped up on the bed and made themselves comfortable right next to me. The process of making myself quiet, breathing evenly, deeply and focusing came easily to me. I had learned to expect anything. Within a minute after I closed my eyes my consciousness moved through a three dimensional darkness that gradually transformed into light. It was often milky white, the kind associated with thick fog. On this evening, the fog gradually dissipated revealing a group of people standing and looking straight at me. They looked like a box of crayons! I couldn't make out all of their faces but all were different colors: almost white, high yellow, butterscotch, café au lait, rich brown with red undertones, burnt umber, chocolate. They reminded me of Papa's family, a spectrum of hues and shades. There were two women, one very fair and tall, the other deep brown and small. I could barely make out their faces.

I asked, "Who are you?"

They all smiled and a man stepped forward from the back who looked like Tony's twin but I knew he wasn't. He was older. Seconds later another man came forward and coaxed the small, deep brown skinned woman to step forward. Although I couldn't make out his face, I knew that was Tony from the way he moved. I had no idea who this woman was. Despite their difference in color, I could see her features and knew she was related to Tony. I just didn't know how. Then they all began to vanish, one at a time, until the only one left was Tony. He looked directly at me and I heard him say, "We've got to hurry. C'mon." And then he was gone.

Instantly I saw a pair of small sandaled feet rushing towards me. I knew it was a woman because of the size of her feet, and the hem of what I thought was a long, chiffon gown. It wasn't a ball gown. This garment was worn by women during ancient times. She extended her hand. I reached for it and left my body to go with her. Her identity was hidden from my memory for quite some time. When her identity was revealed during another meditation, I was told she was or is, "the Eternal You." Reluctantly, I brought myself back to this realm, to consciousness and went to bed.

CHAPTER NINE

The Omega & Alpha

Summer 2007

Summer could be ugly in New York. It wasn't just hot. There could be days when it was humid, sticky, the air cluttered with fumes of all kinds including body odor that blossomed in tight quarters, subways, buses, elevators. To make matters worse, I hated air conditioning. I could tolerate the humidity. I think humidity was invented on the Gulf Coast! Stickiness was unpleasant but not the end of the world for me. It was the air quality I couldn't stand. I heard that little voice again. Only this time the message was different. Instead of advising me to leave the city, I heard, "You have to leave New York." Leave and go where, I wondered? "Did that mean leave the country place also? And why? What's different now that hasn't been? I felt like the city was slowly choking me but I've always managed to cope.

Lucinda would come down to clean for me. I hated housework but I also hated dirt. Dusting, polishing, vacuuming, unloading the dishwasher, all of it made me a little crazy. Often I was afraid to clean out the refrigerator. Science experiments lurked in forgotten containers of food, all green and fuzzy. What I needed were some fresh flowers in the house and I could ignore anything. I realized I was fortunate to have all this done for me. It allowed me to focus on creating a new work life for myself. Politics was out. I had to figure out how to use my creative abilities in the arts to earn enough to compensate what I still received from my inheritance.

I was also contending with nagging problems resulting from Tina's estate. She had died in 1999. There were so many forms to file and those evil estate taxes that had to be paid. I remember signing a check with so many zeros to the federal government I almost fainted. Thankfully she had a wonderful attorney I could rely on to handle her estate and related matters. Years later it felt like she was still among the living, reaching out from the grave attempting to control. She had stashed away money in accounts no one ever knew about. Every now and then I would get a letter from some bank where she had stashed a small pile of money. I was grateful that I could pick up the phone and call her attorney.

The heat of New York City didn't make coping with this any easier. But Lucinda did. She kept reminding me how crazy Tina was and I should go ahead and live my life.

I spent too much time, from my perspective, thinking about Tony and this silliness that was going on between us. It was more than some mindless flirtation but how much more? There were times when he looked at me and I felt like he was undressing me with his eyes. There was more going on than lust. But I couldn't deny the way he looked at me nor the way I looked at him when he wasn't watching. I wanted to yell at him and say, "Look, I'm a size four on most days, maybe a six. There's not a lot here!" It was a nice, playful feature but there was something else. I did believe that whatever this connection was between us would reveal itself. It was amazing how much information about *ourselves* we had revealed to each other. Every encounter was like reading another page in the books of our lives. I was driven to know how long our book was going to be.

Tony Carter had as many opinions as I did. I was delighted by that because we were usually on the same side but I was also thrilled by the comfort of it. I made the mistake of mentioning one well known elected official to him and it was like watching dynamite explode, or race horses tearing out of the gate. He often reminded me of a Palomino horse. His passion was eloquent. I loved it and began to admit that I was falling in love with him.

Having been paid to have opinions by one of the local television stations I rarely encountered someone (outside of the business of politics and media) who had as many opinions as I did but more importantly, he was an ally. I didn't feel alone. Tony and I usually landed on the same side but through radically different routes. His positions and thoughts on issues were the intellectual equivalent of "BOOM!" He was skilled at leaving me speechless but interested. His potential for ranting was high and I enjoyed it. As a woman who worked in traditionally male dominated fields, I couldn't afford to be overtly passionate or as emotional as Tony was. It was too risky. I always had to build my arguments, justify every position. My recommendations for those I worked for too often had to come from my head, not my heart. That's what was expected and that's what I delivered although there's a lot of room in politics to act on "instinct" or to follow your gut especially in electoral politics.

What I did for those I worked for in television and politics often went far beyond the job description. Too often, my job title in politics included the phrase, "Special Aide." That specialness allowed me to clean up messes when my advice was ignored, translate cultural differences among constituencies, and witness the minutia of making history and how easily it could be buried or ignored.

Sometimes I felt like I was deceiving Tony because I never told him about my political work, never told him that some of the politicians he talked about I had worked for, never told him about the television producing, never told him about teaching. I was concerned that he would be intimidated and pull back or treat me differently. Other times I realized he had googled me, so who was I kidding? Maybe he already knew.

We talked about the movie Gladiator and why I was addicted to it. For me Gladiator was about faith, loyalty and justice. I gave Tony my version of Gladiator, helping him first appreciate the uniqueness of Marcus Aurelius, the philosopher king or Cesar. Maximus, who later became the Gladiator, was the General of the Roman army during the reign of Marcus Aurelius. Maximus laid his life down for *a vision, an idea* that Marcus Aurelius had about Rome remaining a Republic. That idea cost him and Maximus their lives.

Maximus died for that *idea,* for what Marcus Aurelius believed in, the ultimate wisdom of the people carried out through the Republic. Maximus paid a price for his loyalty. His wife and son were brutally murdered after Cesar or Marcus Aurelius was murdered by his son. I had been staring off into space while saying all this and more. I went on talking about how the big issues like freedom, justice, honor, democracy had a power all their own that demanded you take a stand. That was comparatively easy.

I wanted Tony to know the little stuff that would get you in today's world. The compromising, not giving in to "the perks of power" for your own good, not knowing what *your price* is (and it's true we all have one), being too tired to continue fighting with an Executive Producer who cuts a scene here, cuts a scene there, and before you know it you end up with something or someone you don't recognize much less care about. The list is endless. This is the stuff that eats you up a day at a time until one morning you wake up, and have no idea who you are or what you've become. That's the real danger. When I did finish, Tony was staring at me with a little bit of joy and amazement.

It was the perfect opening to tell him right then about my work in politics but I didn't. I was scared. The thought of having him pull away or start treating me like I was some kind of hot house flower was more than I could bare. The right time would come I thought. If we could only sit down and have a leisurely conversation, maybe go over to Zabar's or one of those café's on Broadway, then I could lay it all out for him.

I could tell him how I walked away from a very important job because the hypocrisy and micro aggressions in the office were too much. Probably the dumbest thing I ever did professionally but I wanted to leave so my boss and I could still respect each other before we reached the point of no return. It was a heartbreaking experience.

Maybe that's why I didn't tell Tony. Maybe I didn't want to shatter the image of this particular politician, or maybe I didn't want to tell Tony that my first day on the job, as I was looking out the window of my office, I saw black drapes slowly descend around me, and knew right then I had made a terrible mistake and there was no way out of it. I was now confronting required suffering. I knew I had to ride this out. It was meant to be for some reason just as Tony and I were meant to be. It was unavoidable. I had a lesson to learn. As some of my Native American contacts would say, "There's a great teaching taking place."

Tony stood there thinking for a few seconds before saying anything. Measuring every word he said, "I don't know if I could die for an idea."

I looked back at him and said, "Yes you could. Maximus did, in the movie Gladiator..."

"I know *you* could," he said as if he was wandering through my head! "How many times have you seen this movie? Most women have a hard time watching Gladiator."

I hesitated. "Umm – I'll admit to twenty..." I made a face at Tony expressing how incredulous that was.

"Wow," Tony said.

"I know. It's bad. I've seen it so many times there're parts of the dialogue I have memorized!"

He lowered his head to look at me and said, "Really?"

"Yeah," I said. "Listen, hopefully I can remember it all, but this is one of my favorite scenes. It was in the Coliseum after Maximus had been enslaved as a Gladiator. He turned and looked at Marcus Aurelius' son, who assassinated his father to become Cesar, and said, 'My name is Maximus Decimus Meridius, Commander of the Armies of the North, General of the Felix Legions, loyal servant to the true emperor, Marcus Aurelius. Father to a murdered son, husband to a murdered wife. And I will have my vengeance, in this life or the next!' To be strong in the face of adversity, confronting death on your own terms, that's what impressed me. *Oh I loved that scene!*" I twirled around with excitement and felt Tony staring at me charmed. I stopped and said, "I love the movie."

"I can see that," Tony said. "Any other scenes?"

"Yeah, there's a heart breaking scene between Marcus Aurelius and his son, Comidus. After Marcus Aurelius tells him he's going to make Maximus the next Cesar, and all these other qualities Maximus has that make him worthy of being a ruler, his son pleads with him to acknowledge his skills that make him worthy of being Cesar. Marcus Aurelius gets on his knees and tells his son that his faults as son are his failures as a father. It broke my heart watching that scene. The only other line that's stuck with me says 'What we do in life echoes in eternity.' Look, I don't have a crush on Maximus, okay? I wanted to *be* Maximus."

Tony's eyes widened. "Who else in the movies do you want to be like?"

"You doing a survey?" I asked.

He laughed and said, "No, I'm just curious."

"Hmph...okay...the only other character I wanted to be like was Yoda."

"Yoda? Of Star Wars?"

"Yoda," I repeated.

Tony rubbed his hand across his mouth and said, "You are one interesting woman. Look...' he started.

I cut him off and said, "I know, you gotta go." Spike, Yoko and I turned, started to walk away and waved to him over my shoulder.

It was almost ten o'clock and I had put on my pajamas. Tony Carter was going to drive me to drink! I flopped down on the couch with Yoko on one side and Spike on the other and watched television. Yoko suddenly lifted her head. The next thing I heard was someone knocking at the door. It had to be someone from the building otherwise the doorman would've buzzed me.

Yoko and Spike jumped down and ran to the front door barking. I looked through the peephole. I was shocked. It was Tony.

"Just a minute," I yelled and ran into my bedroom. I found my robe, threw it on and went back to the front door. How did he get in? I took a deep breath, exhaled and calmed the spaniels before opening the door. Maybe something happened. I opened the door and said, "Hi. What's wrong?"

He said nothing and walked in. The spaniels sniffed him and stopped barking while I closed the door.

"Tony, how did you get in? Is the doorman not downstairs?" Tony seemed really calm. He looked at me and smiled, cupped my face in his hands and kissed me.

When he stopped, he stepped back and smiled. "Do you know how long I've wanted to do *that*?"

I was dazed and heard myself asking, "Tony, who knows you're here?"

Reaching for me, he said, "You do and that's all that matters." He kissed me again. I had no idea how much this night would matter.

Manhattan was experiencing a miserable summer day. I knew this kind of heat was an outgrowth of climate change just as I knew when the first plane hit the World Trade Tower that it was terrorism and not some misguided, lost pilot who didn't see the building!

People were sticking to the sidewalks. Tempers were short. Even Spike and Yoko were walking a little slower. Down the block we went passing some other dog owners nodding and making small talk about the weather, the news, and the endless construction going on in Manhattan. As a child I remembered the Con Edison phrase plastered everywhere, "Dig We Must." The digging and construction continue.

It was a little past 6 PM. Summer had officially arrived a few days earlier but the weather delivered the heat long before. Common sense forced me to put on a pair of denim shorts, a tee-shirt and sandals. As usual, my hair felt out of control, but it wasn't. I had it radically cut for manageability. My beautician wanted me to consider dying my hair to cover the silver and white hairs that were taking over, obliterating the jet black masses of curls. I said no. There were too many people who considered it my trademark. Even Tony had commented, thinking it was a rouse so people would get confused about my age. The truth was I was too lazy and too cheap to spend hundreds of dollars every month on my hair! Anyway, I liked confusing people.

As we turned the corner, someone ran by me and briefly slipped their arm around my waist. It was a very smooth move and for a second or two all of us were jogging along until he let go of my waist. It was Tony.

"Whoa," I said! "Where are you going? Slow down."

He turned to face me and continued to run backwards as if he was playing basketball, but at a slower pace. "I'm late. I've got to take these people out."

"Out? Out where?" I asked. "What people?" I'd never seen him this rushed. At the same time I remembered him playing basketball several weeks ago. I saw him walking down the street one day bouncing a basketball and noticed a Band-Aid over his left eyebrow. Alarmed, I pointed to it.

He said, "Basketball."

"Okay," I replied. I never thought of basketball as a violent sport but it could get rough.

In unison we said, "Fighting off old age!"

Coming back to the present, I heard Tony say, "My boat. Every year I take out some people from work. Remember, I told you that last night?"

Was it possible to be jealous of a boat? I pushed that out of my mind. It made me feel childish. It's just a boat and then I remembered when he told me and how he told me. It was a miracle. I finally got him to stop for more than five minutes!

By now he had reached his car. He stopped for a minute and looked at me. "When I come back, we're going out," he said. "Dinner? Brunch? Whatever you want," he yelled. *"We have a lot to talk about, right?"* He looked at me and I looked at him as he gazed at me before starting his car. We had some intense conversations with our eyes. I had never experienced anything like that with anyone else.

I felt my face light up at the prospect of really talking with this man as he drove away. I looked down at Spike and Yoko, and said, "Did you hear that? We're going out! We're going to talk like grownups. Finally!"

As he drove away, I felt a brief sense of frustrated victory. I almost skipped home singing in my head, "You bring me joy..." I didn't care if he was seeing anybody else because as of yesterday when we had our encounter, they were now toast, cooked, done, gone! Wait until I tell Kae, I thought.

As soon as I fed Spike and Yoko, I combed through my CDs and pulled out the original version of "You're All I Need To Get By." It made me smile. I kept saying to myself, yes, yes, yes! I found the Alicia Keys recording that was haunting Tony and me, "Everything's Going to Be All Right." It is now, I believed, because Tony said when he comes back we're going out! I said that out loud to Spike and Yoko and Yoko barked back at me. I wasn't an opera fan but there were some arias that really moved me and one of those was Con Te Partiro, the loose translation being, "Time to Say Goodbye." For me, music was the most magical of the arts. I put all three on the CD player, leaned back on the couch to enjoy the new possibilities between Anthony Jacob Ian Carter, III, and myself, Spike and Yoko.

The evening slowly unfolded. The air was still thick with heat and humidity but a wave of cold washed over me suddenly. As quickly as it came it left. Maybe five minutes later, it happened again. My first thought was I was coming down with an annoying summer cold. I got up from the couch and went to fix a cup of tea. As soon as I was in the kitchen, the spaniels started to bark. I rushed back to the living room and found them barking at the Eames lounge chair. I looked at the chair and then at them, motioning for quiet. They stopped barking but continued staring at the chair. Spike began to circle the chair and wagged his tail. Yoko had jumped up on the couch and watched the chair, smiling, mouth open, and tongue hanging half way out. I didn't like it and I ignored what I sensed. I walked back to the kitchen and experienced another chill. "What is going on?" I asked myself.

I went to bed thinking about all the possibilities that waited for Tony and me. The places we could go. The things we would see. The fun that sat poised when Christmas came to Fifth Avenue, the red bow around the Cartier's building, Rockefeller Center, the magical store windows. I wondered if he had ever been to Paris. I knew I was getting ahead of myself but I didn't care.

Evening became night. Spike and Yoko were in bed next to me, cuddled up, ready for sleep. I turned out the light but still felt cold. I pulled up a light weight comforter and refused to think about why I was feeling cold. Just as I drifted off to sleep, I heard the spaniels bark once or twice. I felt them move to the foot of the bed and I sensed the presence of someone else.

The next morning after walking Spike and Yoko, I sat down at my desk and went online to check my emails. It was later than usual for me, close to 9:30 AM. I knew I had missed Tony. He was already at work. I would email him and find out how the boat ride went and remind him that he said we were going out.

The only noise I heard while scanning my emails came from the spaniels. For some reason they were restless. I could hear them moving around in the living room.

I saw an email from Christine. I leaned back in my chair, clicked it open and my life blew up.

"Hey, Janis. I'm going away for a few days but I just thought you should know in case you haven't heard, Tony died yesterday in a boating accident. He drowned. It was on the news last night. I'll call you this evening."

I read that over and over. Time froze. Everything was *not* a blur. It was all too clear. I was barely breathing. I felt disemboweled, gutted like a fish. I was now face to face with a threatening intruder. It was grief, armed and dangerous, a different kind with devastation as a side kick. I was lost. I was enraged. I wanted somebody to pay for this. *"I shall have my vengeance in this life or the next."* Somebody, somewhere had to be responsible.

Everything in my head and heart broke. I sat there and said, "No, no, no…this can't be. There's got to be a mistake." I must have said, no, a hundred times. I had to call somebody. Somebody had to know something, and I started to think about who could possibly have some information. Do I still know anyone in the newsroom of the affiliate stations where I used to work? How do I reach his sister? Where is she? How could Tony drown? That just doesn't make any sense. He couldn't drown! He was so at home in the water. How does that happen? It's got to be wrong but I knew it wasn't.

The spaniels were now barking. I got up and almost fell running to them. They were standing on the ottoman barking and wagging their tails at the empty Eames lounge chair. I watched them for a few minutes and then walked over to calm them down.

"What's the matter? What are you barking at? Come on. Let's go to the kitchen and get some biscuits." They understood biscuits and stopped barking. They followed me into the kitchen. My head was spinning. After they ate, they went right back to the lounge chair still unsettled. I took a deep breath to calm myself, fixed a cup of tea, and went back to my office. I called Lucinda and told her the news.

"What do you mean he's dead?!! Dead how?"

I told her what I knew and she shrieked. "A boat?! What the hell he doing with a boat? He own a boat? Oh, my God. I be right down, Miss Janis. You should not be by yourself."

I didn't think it was necessary for her to come down but she ignored me, thank-God. Kae was my next call. There was a part of me that was dreading this.

"Hello."

"Kae? It's me. I have some bad news," I said.

"What's wrong? You don't sound right. You're not sick, are you?" she asked.

"Kae, it's Tony."

Kae was silent for a few seconds. "Janis, don't tell me something's happened to that man."

"Tony died yesterday in a boating accident."

There was silence and then Kae stuck a knife in my heart when she said, "Oh Lord. Janis, this is your fault! You should've gone after that man sooner. I told you to do that! The minute he spoke to you, you needed to grab him."

"Kae, what was I supposed to do?"

"You could've done something instead of waiting on him! You could've kept him off that boat. Now that poor man is dead and you're left. You're not going to find anyone else like him."

My head felt like it was going to explode again. "Kae, I couldn't stop him. He's a grown man. He loved sailing. He wasn't going to stop and he wasn't going to give up his friends either."

"Life changes in a minute, and the Lord meant for the two of you to be together. Lord have mercy"

"There was nothing I could do. I didn't control Tony."

"Well, we'll never know now. But he was the one," Kae said.

I don't know how we ended the conversation, but we did. I went and sat in the living room with Spike and Yoko next to me, and waited for Lucinda to arrive. I tried not to think about anything. It didn't work. Every conversation Tony and I had played in my head, every smile, every frown, every flirtatious moment and that one special encounter the day before he went sailing, I didn't want to tell anyone about it, not Kae, not Lucinda and certainly not his sister. Lucinda walked in maybe two hours later. The spaniels ran towards her barking and wagging their tails.

"Oh my God," Lucinda said. She dropped her overnight bag by the front door and then rushed over to me. "I'm so sorry." She stared at me and her eyes narrowed. "Miss Janis, say something."

I looked up and focused on her before speaking, "Something's not right. I think Tony's here."

Lucinda sat down next to me, "What do you mean?"

"I can feel him." I pointed to the lounge chair and said, "I think he was sitting right there earlier and shortly after he died yesterday. I had gotten so cold and the spaniels started to bark then and this morning. He's been here."

Lucinda sighed, "Okay. Look I'm going to fix you a fresh cup of tea and walk Yoko and Spike. You should go to bed. If you have anywhere to go today, cancel it. We get through this. You, me, Yoko, Spike and God, we get through this. I'm going nowhere."

As soon as Lucinda left with Spike and Yoko, I leaned back on the couch and saw an image of Tony being engulfed by waves. The waves embraced him, pulling him, luring him under and he went around and around in the water, swaddled by the currents. This image stayed with me. Almost six years later, I was attending an Easter Vigil service at Tony's church. I heard the priest speak of water as a conduit for resurrection. I saw Tony rising from the water that took his life. Tony didn't give up but gave in to the water's force and rose again. He passed from life to death to life.

Drained, I did go to bed earlier than usual that evening. My head hit the pillow and tears slid from my eyes. Just as I was drifting off, I felt Spike and Yoko move to the foot of the bed. I turned over and for a moment I saw Tony in some ethereal form lying in bed next to me. I could make out this face, his torso, the arms and his arms. The rest of him was light, and I heard him say, "Don't worry. Stop crying. I'm never going to leave you."

I woke up the next morning and found Spike and Yoko back in their usual places next to me. Squinting at the clock on my nightstand, it said 6:30 AM. The spaniels had to be walked. After brushing my teeth and washing my face, I quickly dressed and we walked down the hall and into the kitchen. I saw Lucinda looking out the window.

"Lucinda?"

She turned around. Her face said it all. Her eyes were wide with disbelief and awe. Whispering, she said, "Yes…"

"What happened? Are you okay?" I asked and filled Spike and Yoko's bowls with fresh water. I vacillated from feeling numb to being enraged and now concerned about Lucinda. I sat the bowls down and looked at her. "What's going on? Tell me."

Holding her hands, she said, "I think I saw Mr. Tony…"

I rubbed my hand across my forehead and said, "Where Lucinda? How?" I leaned against a kitchen counter so I wouldn't collapse, and waited.

"Your room. Last night after you went to bed I looked in on you... There was this man in the bed next to you. I knew it was Mr. Tony. I never met him, but I knew it was him. He was... I don't know how to describe it, but I know what I saw."

I didn't know what to say to her so I hugged her. "I'm going to walk Spike and Yoko."

"I can do that," she said.

"No, I need to get some air," I said. Automatically the spaniels and I walked our usual route. We turned the corner and walked down Tony's block. I didn't know how I was going to do this day after day now that he was gone. His doorman waved at me. We stopped and he told me how sad he was about Tony's death. I looked at the doorman and agreed that it was sad.

"The two of you had something going, didn't you?"

"What makes you say that?" I asked.

"C'mon...I watched the two of you. He'd come out in the morning and wait for you to turn that corner like clockwork. I think he fell for you," the doorman said and smiled. "He was a good man, caring man. I'm gonna miss him. You know, the two of you looked related. Anybody ever tell you that?"

"No," I said. I was surprised.

"Kinda cute," the doorman said and smiled.

I smiled back. "You have a good day."

"You too. I'm sorry for your loss." The spaniels and I continued our walk. I kept thinking about the absurdity of all this.

We got back and Lucinda was wiping down the kitchen counters. I fed Spike and Yoko and then started to fix breakfast for myself. I was hesitant to talk with Lucinda. Pouring a bowl of cereal, I asked, "Do you want to talk about seeing Tony?"

"Miss Janis, God was in that room. I don't know how to explain it, but I do believe in everlasting life and I know what I saw. It was proof for me that there's no ending, no death, just new beginnings. Mr. Tony just somewhere else now. He's not here but he's not dead like we think either. I know you see these things sometimes but I've never seen what I saw, you know? He was glowing or something. Then he faded away. I mean, I know what I saw but I can't tell anybody but you. I would never speak of it. You know how people are. But that to me, what I saw, was a sacred moment. "

I just nodded my head. "I understand."

"What are you going to do?" Lucinda asked.

I looked past her and out the kitchen window before speaking, "I don't know, Lucinda. But I think my life is radically changing in some way." I ate breakfast wondering how I was going to get any information on the service, on his family, on what actually happened. The more I thought about Tony drowning, the less sense it made.

I don't know what led me to call one friend, but I did. She had a friend who was a friend of Tony's sister. By the end of the day, I had his sister's name and address. I held onto that piece of paper. Standing in the living room, the couch caught me as I fell into it. I don't know how long I sat there and stared into space holding on to that piece of paper. Now, it was the most valuable thing I had. It was the only concrete connection I had to Tony.

CHAPTER TEN

That Big Church

I don't know when I did this nor how considering I was in a daze. But I wrote a note to Cathy the day after Tony died. I didn't know how to introduce myself. I didn't know what she knew. I figured she knew something because Tony confided in her, but how much? Did she know about that encounter? Had he talked to her about asking me out? Maybe the woman hated me but I would risk finding that out.

I wanted his sister to know in some small way that I understood the totality of this very specific grief that tears open your heart and leaves you bloodless, stunned, mute and a little crazy. Nothing would ever be the same but you'd be flooded with well-meaning clichés in cards and conversations. "Time heals all wounds. You'll get through this. With time your grief will diminish." I knew these were lies. *This* grief doesn't diminish. It simply changes. It may feel differently, occupy until now unknown spaces in your heart, soul and memory. *This* grief pops up and screams your loss at inconvenient times and in peculiar ways usually when you're surrounded by the wrong people. *This* grief can wrap itself around you like a boa constrictor and render you immobile for a few minutes or a few days, sometimes forever *– but it doesn't go away, and you won't forget, and you will never stop hurting. It will just be different.* And when well meaning, sincere friends say, "Let me know if there's anything I can do," ask them, "Can you bring him back?"

I knew his sister was a person of faith. So my wish for her was the following, "In the days that follow, when all the rituals are done and people have left, may God hold you in His arms and give you comfort and solace." If you weren't a person of faith, *any faith*, I don't know what you do. I really don't, not in the face of an inexpressible loss.

I had lost ten friends important to my well-being mostly to cancer. One was killed by a drunk driver. It was too early for them to die. With each death, a chapter of my life went with them. The friend I needed the most, Bridgett, during this was gone. I was looking for some stationary to write Cathy a note and saw the letter Bridgett's mother had written me. I stopped to read it again. It was a way for me to feel Bridget's closeness.

"For too long I have wanted to write to you – the special dear friend of our dear Bridgett. But I must tell you how truly she valued your long and lasting friendship. She spoke of you often, of the mutual changes in your lives, of her deep affection for Janis. She was always so glad to have you as a friend, sharing her life, sharing moments both delightful and sad. This note is simply to thank you for all the years you offered her support and courage. My memories of her will always include you as her wonderful friend – someone such an important part of her life. I am so grateful for the joys and treasures you gave to her too short life. With much affection and love…"

And now I'd lost Tony who took a chapter that had just begun and was aborted. At least that's what I thought. I stood there not moving, hoping that perhaps Bridgett would meet Tony on the other side.

For me, shock in all its forms became my companion. I was very good at going through the motions of normalcy. I had a radio show to do. I was teaching, writing and painting. Nobody really knew about this "thing" going on between Tony and me except for his doorman and Lucinda! Christine didn't understand either although she was actively suspicious. So, other people would be perplexed. Why would I be upset over the loss of what? What was he to you? We were the only ones who knew what we meant to each other and what we would become.

I sent his sister my letter and found out what the arrangements were.

The service would be held at the big, fancy church in midtown I often walked by while shopping but never entered. Another aspect of my life was about to change.

A few days later when I did enter Tony's church for the first time, I realized he died twenty days before my birthday. I shook my head knowing something was going on.

The magnificence of the church humbled me. It made me still. I was given a program and sat in one of the back pews. People filed in, many of them with faces of disbelief and confusion. Led to the first two pews, the family was seated. I looked, hoping somehow to recognize his sister, Cathy, and then I remembered I had seen them before. I recognized all of them. I was looking at the people I had seen in my box of crayons meditation! Some had distinctive high cheekbones and deeply set roundish eyes that made me think there had to be some Asian ancestry somewhere. All the colors were there: butterscotch, chocolate icing, burnt umber, beige, and the color of egg nog. Tony had shown me Cathy in the meditation. Now she was seated in the first pew.

The service began. All of my abandoned Episcopalian ways came back. I was fine until the casket was rolled in. At times I thought I could see right through it to Tony's body lying there immobile, eternally still, probably wearing something blue. I thought my brain would explode. I closed my eyes to hold back the tears and stop myself from letting out a shattering, impolite, non-Episcopalian scream. I heard the priest say, "Tony, you left us too soon." I didn't know what to do except be thankful he'd been in my life at all.

When I stood for a prayer I heard Tony whisper in my ear, "I'm never going to leave you. I'm here for you." He was standing right next to me and it took my breath away.

"This is our church," he said. I could feel his closeness and I could feel him smile. He touched my hand and I opened mine so he could wrap his hand around mine. For a second I saw him.

A wash of emotion filled my entire being. I was flooded with relief that he wasn't really gone. His presence had a distinctive vibration that I sensed. Even though I saw him for only a second, I felt his hand in mine and that was all I needed, but I also felt slightly dizzy. There was a buzzing or humming sensation I had ignored. I wanted to dance out of the church! Right then I decided to come back to this church because at the very least, I could find Tony's spirit there.

Someone was staring at me and I turned to see who it was. An older, distinguished woman with beautiful white hair, pulled back in a bun, was looking at me with a deep, warm expression. At that instant, I knew that she knew. I knew that somehow she was also seeing Tony. The warmth of Tony's hand began to fade and I noticed that the church was emptying. Time had stopped for me. The service was over and the woman was gone. I looked for her. It seemed like she too vanished.

I looked quickly around and realized the family had left the sanctuary. I rushed outside to find Cathy. I wanted to say something, anything. I just needed to connect with her.

People seemed to be lingering on the steps of the church and sidewalk. They looked lost and bewildered. The disbelief was palpable. I found an usher and asked where was the family. Pointed in the right direction, I made my way to Cathy and introduced myself, saying I had sent her the note. She grabbed my hand and said, "I was wondering who you were." Somebody told me they were going out to the gravesite and I was welcome to follow them. I didn't go. I told them I didn't want to intrude. The truth? I couldn't stand it.

I got home and changed. Spike and Yoko were in the living room, both in the lounge chair and looking quite content. "Hey," I said. They wagged their tails. Spike jumped down and pranced over to me. I gave him a hug. By now, Yoko had joined him.

Once I changed we went for a walk. It was important for me to keep going. Regardless of all the craziness I grew up with, one of the traits passed down was strength. It was important to have strength not only to face threats, violence and discrimination, but to stand up and keep going regardless. Whatever the pain was, keep going. Grief expressed within the circle of my grandparents was often silent. There's a passage in Joseph M. Marshall's book, *Keep Going*, from a Native Elder, Old Hawk, who says, "Life can give you strength. Strength can come from facing the storms of life, from knowing loss, feeling sadness and heartache, from falling into the depths of grief. You must stand up in the storm. You must face the wind and the cold and the darkness. When the storm blows hard you must stand firm, for it is not trying to knock you down, it is really trying to teach you to be strong. Being strong means taking one more step toward the top of the hill, no matter how weary you may be. It means letting the tears flow through the grief. It means keep looking for the answer, though the darkness of despair is all around. Keep going."

Before I knew it, we were on Tony's block. I heard myself say, I don't think I can do this. We turned around and took a different route. When we got back, I sat down in the Eames lounge chair. The spaniels joined me. I leaned back, placed my legs on the ottoman and tried to shut out this ugly, new reality.

"I'm never leaving you."

My eyes flipped open and I shouted, "But you did!"

CHAPTER ELEVEN

Every Day

Tony was in my head every day and in my dreams many nights. Vivid, puzzling dreams with disjointed scenes in high definition. The two of us in different rooms, in wonderful houses located somewhere familiar, designed and laid out in a way that made me think I had furnished them. I had never lost my passion for architecture having studied it in college. The details in these dreams were so specific I started to wonder if I was experiencing dreams at all and maybe this was something different. What I saw was so clear, I could draw the floor plans, indicate where pieces of furniture were placed, and find the exact color of the walls. There were six framed photos of sailboats over the living room fireplace. What I couldn't do was see more than was shown to me.

Every day, at some point, I asked Tony, "Why did you have to leave?" I just didn't understand. Something was very wrong.

Thankfully I had Spike and Yoko and Lucinda. I spent more time working with oil and chalk pastels, and more time in the country. The ache from his loss led me to create countless abstract chalk pastel compositions, most of them primarily in blue, all shades, all sizes. (Blue was Tony's favorite color.) This was the only activity that made any sense to me. The volume and intensity of the work had a different impact on Lucinda. She walked in the studio one day and slowly scanned the room. She looked at the larger pieces longer than the smaller ones. Leaning over my shoulder as I worked on a smaller one I could feel her breathing.

"Miss Janis, who's going to see these? What are you going to do with all these?"

Continuing to work, I said, "I don't know."

"You need to do something. They're beautiful. They make you think they're breathing, alive, something. I know you know art people. *Somebody needs to see this.*"

I turned to look at her and said, "Maybe. Maybe I'll show some to his sister one day. But why would she talk to me, Lucinda?"

Lucinda was scanning my work again and muttered, "Oh my God," and left.

I smiled and continued to work.

Several days later I went to the city to do my radio show, spend a night or two, and then returned to the country. I wondered what Tony would've thought of this place. The peace of open, green spaces became more appealing and soothing as time went on. But I couldn't shake my need for book stores, Fifth Avenue, Zabar's and museums yet.

A new reality evolved for me. Tony was a constant presence. We don't have the language to describe paranormal and spiritual phenomenon accurately. If I said, "The atmosphere gets tight" when he's around or, "The air changes," who would understand? "The energy changes," or, "The air feels crowded or compressed," who would grasp or recognize the situation? One thing was certain, I wasn't alone. I knew it and the spaniels knew it. Lucinda pretended she knew nothing! Christine was terrified every time I mentioned it, so I stopped. It was just me and Tony. I started to live in two worlds, mine in this dimension on earth, and the dimension on the other side of the veil. That dimension is as complex and varied, if not more, than this life on earth. Holding all this is exhausting. Aside from learning how to manage what I saw on any given day, I had intuitively developed some ethical standards regarding the information I received. It wasn't necessary to tell or use everything I sensed about a person, nor what I saw.

Parking my car while visiting a friend in Westchester, I managed to slam the car door on my right forefinger. It was a pain so horrific that it left me voiceless. I thought I had broken it. The next day I went to the Infirmary at the radio station to get a finger splint. Whether I broke it or not was irrelevant according to the nurse. My finger needed to be immobile, regardless, hence the splint. Holding my right hand up, (because it hurt less) I walked back to my office really angry with myself for being so careless.

"Want me to kiss it and make it feel better?"

I slowed down, looked around and the hall was empty. Who said that? Then I sensed someone was chuckling. It was Tony. I felt it in every bone of my body. It almost took my breath away. I looked around again to make sure no one else was there. Just me... and Tony. For a second, out of the corner of my eye I saw him standing next to me, hands in his pockets with a mischievous grin on his face.

When I returned to my office, the Station Manager reminded me of the staff outing the next day. Our annual bonding event! I didn't pay close attention to what he was saying because I had no interest in it. The fact that it was the next day never stayed in my mind.

The next day came and promptly at noon, the Station Manager marched into my office and said, "Let's go. It's time."

Perplexed, I looked up and said, "Go where?"

"The staff outing! Come on, let's go," he said and walked out.

I found some of my colleagues at the elevator and asked one of them, "Where the hell are we going?"

"He's chartered a boat for us. We'll circle Manhattan like tourists, have some lunch, a drink or two, get back and go home early. Let the computers run the station."

"We're going on a boat ride?" I repeated.

"Yeah, what's wrong?"

My stomach sank. I was terrified of getting on boats. They were never flush with the dock leaving a couple of inches where you could see the water. I was convinced I would fall through that space and drown. The last thing I ever wanted to do was take a boat ride, especially now. All boats were now condemned as far as I was concerned. It was a damned boat that took Tony away from me.

We stood on the dock, making small talk while waiting for the boat. The Operations Manager walked over and asked, "Are you okay? You look... funny."

I liked her. She had a great sense of humor and we both had a deep appreciation for shoes! I studied her for a few seconds before saying anything, "You know, I lost someone to a boat accident almost a year ago. I'm not big on boats."

"Why didn't you tell me? I would've found a way for you to get out of this."

"It's okay. I'll survive," I said as I watched the boat arrive. People started getting in line. Slowly I walked towards the boat, looked down and saw the approaching gap. Oh Jesus, I thought. How am I going to do this? The last time I was in a predicament like this was leaving the command station of the Panama Canal while covering a Presidential campaign. Those huge gates would open and close allowing boats to slip through. Who knew that when the gates closed to form a narrow foot bridge they weren't flush in the middle? There had to be almost a six inch gap! I survived with the help of a cameraman walking in front of me and a sound man walking in back of me. How was I going to survive this? The person in front of me got on the boat. It was my turn and I could barely breathe, much less lift my feet.

"Come on. Don't worry. I won't let you fall."

I was so startled by Tony's voice, I leaped on board.

Everyone else went into the main cabin. I dropped into the first seat I could find on the deck. The boat pulled away and went pushing its way through the Hudson River headed to the most northern point of Manhattan to veer east into the East River going south. The air was warm, and I could feel the soft spray of water sprinkle my face. I took some deep breaths and started thinking about the absurdity of Tony drowning.

The Operations Manager came out of the cabin. She sat down next to me and asked, "Are you okay?"

I looked out at the water for a moment before answering her. "I'm going to be fine. Give me some time. I'll be in soon."

"Okay. They haven't started serving lunch yet, but once they do..."

I nodded my head and she went back to the cabin. Staring at the water, I dozed off. My head dropped and bounced back. I opened my eyes, looking up and saw Tony, sailing. He had on the most sparkling white polo shirt I'd ever seen. It was dazzling but not blinding. And he had on a pair of khaki cargo Bermuda shorts. He looked so happy. It was so vivid, so real. Within seconds the image faded. I wanted to get off the boat but I was stuck there for over an hour.

When we returned, I got in my car and headed towards the West Side Highway. I just wanted to curl into a ball and sleep for as long as possible. While waiting for the light to turn green my hand rested on the gear shift. The light turned green. I put my foot on the gas and what happened next was almost imperceptible. There was a hand on top of mine and then a gentle squeeze. I took a deep breath, let it out slowly, and was thankful I didn't drive into another car or the Hudson River!

I parked the car and took the elevator to my floor. As I rode up, I thought, I don't know if I can do this. I don't know if I can hold all this. Maybe I'm having a breakdown. I wanted to believe that but I knew it wasn't true. I opened the door and Yoko and Spike were right there to greet me. Numb, I took them for a walk, came back and we all ate. I sat in the living room until it got dark, then took the spaniels out one more time around ten PM. Returning, we went straight to my bedroom and turned on the television. Instead of being relaxed by television, I became tense and distracted. As I undressed and got ready for bed, I started talking out loud to Tony.

"What do you want me to know? That you're still here? You've made your point." Wrapped in my pajamas, I sat on the foot of the bed staring into nothing. Eventually I got up and walked into my bathroom and washed my face. While rubbing cream on it, I looked in the mirror and saw something glowing, formed like a human, standing behind me. I dropped the face cream, turned around and saw nothing. Thankfully, the jar of cream had not shattered. I put the jar back in the medicine cabinet, turned out the bathroom light and went back to my bedroom. There was nothing, just Spike and Yoko sleeping at the foot of the bed.

I sat on my bed and closed my eyes. I started to breathe slowly and deliberately. After a few seconds, I heard myself say,

"Tony, you're here aren't you?" I waited. Nothing. I opened my eyes and got in bed. The television turned itself off. Then my bedside lamp flickered on and off several times before I was in complete darkness. I tried not to panic. I leaned back and sat cross-legged in bed. Spike and Yoko were sound asleep.

"Tony, what do you want me to do? Tell me before I flip out, please."

"*I want you to go to bed.*"

"Tony, I'm in bed."

"*No, I want you to lie down and get under the covers. I need to show you something. Don't worry.*"

I felt helpless but I did what he said and waited. I was on the edge of sleep when I felt something so familiar but so radically different at the same time. It was the emotion of intimacy that I recognized but the rest... My body began to tingle. It started with my feet. It was as if every inch of me was being awakened by this flickering sensation, like very mild electric shocks opening little doors in my body. When every door was opened we connected at the speed of light. I felt weightless, ethereal, sparkling all over. That's when I realized I had somehow merged with Tony so completely I was breathless. The fulfillment couldn't be described in words. I didn't want it to end.

I heard Tony ask, "*You okay?*"

"I'm okay," I whispered.

The last thing I remembered seeing before I fell asleep was Tony next to me.

The next morning when I woke up the television was on, my lamp was on and Spike and Yoko were next to me.

Lying there, I asked myself, "Was last night real? Please let it be real and not my imagination."

"*It wasn't your imagination.*"

Overwhelmed doesn't begin to describe how I was feeling. I called Kae and told her I needed to talk to her about some things that have happened since Tony died.

"Stop saying he died. He just passed over to the other side," Kae said.

"I'm still hearing from him and even seeing him in one form or another. I'm living in two worlds. It's exhausting. I know he's right here now, listening to us. Am I losing my mind?" I asked knowing that I wasn't.

"No baby, you're not losing your mind." Kae reminded me that Mama, who was her aunt, and Tina had this gift.

"Your grandmother's father also had it," Kae said.

"I've only heard bits and pieces," I said.

"Um-hmm. Then your grandfather had all those Indians in his family. You're the latest recipient. You've had it all your life."

"Well, what did Mama and Tina do with it?"

Kae sighed heavily. "Your childhood was more complicated than a ball of tangled yarn. Your grandmother used her gift to heal. She also knew how to pray with power. When your grandmother prayed for anyone, watch out! That's how she protected herself when the Klan was a daily reality. It's how she protected you from that jackass who was your father. You've had some really close calls but you're still here."

My mind flashed back to the time when my father held a knife to my throat. How I wiggled away from him was a miracle. That was one time when being small worked to my advantage. I was hard to hold on to. And then there was the time he pushed Tina onto a fifth story window ledge at an apartment she leased, thinking she was going to be on her own, out from under her parents' rule. She dragged me there for a weekend. It didn't work. Harry threatened to push her off the ledge. I was eight or nine. I called the police and locked myself in a room by jamming a chair under the door knob. When the police arrived, Tina explained that she was a professional woman not some average person. I never went back to her apartment and she eventually returned to the brownstone, defeated, with her husband in tow.

"Close calls because of Tina," I said.

"Oh girl, you don't know the half of it.," Kae said.

"I figured that," I mumbled. "Now Kae, I know you have this gift. You *are* Mama's niece."

"Sometimes I can just feel things. That's all."

I smiled, said good-bye and hung up.

My grief wasn't easing. It was transforming into a deep ache. There were days when I could feel Tony passing through as if to make sure things were okay. There were evenings when I knew he was looking at me watch television while Spike and Yoko acknowledged his presence with a gentle bark and wag of their tails. Then there were several days in a row when I knew he was busy, away, doing things. I had a vague sense of him learning things and I wanted to know what those things were. These were comfortable sensations and over time became as familiar to me as the air I breathe.

But there were other times when the air around me felt heavy and charged. I remember opening the door late one afternoon when Yoko and Spike didn't come running. I was alarmed. They always greeted me when I came home. I walked very quietly into the living room. I didn't know what I would find but I knew we weren't in any danger.

Spike and Yoko were on the couch, chins resting on their front paws, looking directly at the lounge chair. Yoko slowly wagged her tail a few times. Neither one of them looked at me. I was afraid to breathe. I thought I would disturb some invisible energy field that seemed to consume the living room. There was that faint, familiar buzzing sensation like a low key hum, much in the same way a refrigerator sounds. It made me think that the atmosphere had been reconfigured or recharged. I walked over to the couch and sat down next to them. They didn't move. I sat with them until "it" left. The low key hum seemed to dissipate. That's when I leaned back on the couch and started to breathe at a normal rate. I looked at Spike and Yoko and said, "He was here, wasn't he?" Spike looked at me as if to say, "What do you think?"

I changed clothes. Put on some jeans and found an oversized white shirt. Some friends called this my uniform. As I looked for some shoes, the spaniels joined me. Spike ran into my closet and carried out a pair of yellow, suede ballet flats and dropped them in front of my bed. Why not? I slid my feet into them and off we went for our walk. I half expected to see Tony at the corner, or the end of the block, or right next to me!

That happened the following week.

I was leaving the radio station. There was a long hall that led to the elevators designated for the garage. Just as I turned the corner I saw him. Tony was standing in front of the elevators holding a baby girl in his arms. He was beaming with happiness. The little girl had on a pink dress or coat. She couldn't have been more than a year old. It was her hair that made the biggest impression on me. It was a massive mop of black curls. I had stopped walking mesmerized by both of them. They faded from sight and I began walking again. I needed to talk to Kae. I had told her what I saw on the boat ride. She was so overcome with emotion she almost cried. Wait until she heard this.

Kae told me that it was time to honor the gift God gave me.

"I don't know what to do with it. I'm certainly not a psychic who gives readings. That's not what I do."

Kae said. "It'll show itself. Now you listen to me, you and Sailor Man are not finished. I know that and so do you."

The following Friday morning I was leaving the city for the country and decided to visit Tony's grave on the way. The first anniversary of his death was approaching. I'd been avoiding this but I needed to see where his family had put him. I needed to do something! The spaniels and I headed up to Putnam County where the cemetery was located. Upon arriving, I received a map with the location of his grave site circled and a vague set of driving directions. The cemetery was small and beautifully landscaped with narrow lanes requiring you to drive slowly. I passed several small chapels before arriving at his grave site. Lowering the car windows, I left Spike and Yoko and walked over to Tony's headstone. Standing in front of it, I was aware of birds flying overhead. I looked over my shoulder just in time to see an owl glide by my car. As he went on his way, I said out loud, "You've been trying to talk to me. I didn't pay attention. I'm sorry."

Someone had put fresh flowers on Tony's grave. I reached inside my pocket, pulled out a seashell, and placed it in front of the headstone.

"I had to see where they put you," I said. "I couldn't come after the service." I sat cross-legged on his grave for almost a half hour and stared at the headstone, grateful that he had come into my life and devastated he'd left so soon. I told him, "When you finally spoke to me I knew my life was never going to be the same. There was something joyful and playful in your eyes, and I knew, in that way women know, that you and I would spend our lives together. My heart was open. My hands were open. I was ready to welcome you into my life." Sitting there I lost sense of time. When I looked at my watch, I saw that over an hour had passed. I got up, wiped away some tears, pulled out a tissue from my pocket and blew my nose. I walked back to my car. I wanted to get to the country before it was dark.

I saw Spike and Yoko looking just beyond me and I felt a presence behind me. When I looked over my shoulder, I saw a stream of golden flecks following me. I was awestruck. There was a beauty about these flecks that brought a smile to my face. They seemed to be alive and went with me into the car and filled it. The spaniels were enchanted. I had no idea what anyone else saw. Frankly, I was scared to look at drivers passing by. The car held these flecks all the way to the house and inside to the living room.

I collapsed on the living room couch, leaned back and watched these golden flecks fill the room. It was magical and amazing. They seemed to have individual lives as they danced and twinkled. At one point I thought these flecks were breathing. They were alive in a way I didn't understand. Sometimes they clustered, wrapping me in their light. Spike and Yoko stood in the middle of the floor trying to catch them. When they realized it was futile, they jumped up on the couch next to me. There was a hypnotic quality to these flecks. One by one, they gradually disappeared. I heard myself say, "Wow."

I looked at the spaniels and said, *"I've got to call Cathy.* She has to know about this, all of it." I had her work number and her home address written down somewhere. It took me a few minutes to locate it.

I called her at work, and reintroduced myself. She said, "Oh, I know who you are." I didn't know if that was a good thing or a bad thing. "Listen, I've got to talk to you. I know this sounds crazy but I've *really got to talk to you*. I can come to you or, if you like, I'd be happy to have you come to my place in the city. I'll be back in a few days."

"Okay," she said. "I know where you live."

I was taken aback by her response. How did she know where I lived? I assumed Tony told her. We confirmed a date and time. Cathy would come by next week.

At the exact time and place, Cathy showed up at the apartment, and received an enthusiastic greeting from the spaniels. They calmed down and trotted into the living room with Cathy behind them. She looked around and commented on all my books. "You know, Tony would've loved this, all these books."

I smiled and asked if I could get her some tea or wine – anything. She said no and sat down.

"I know this is going to sound crazy and I'm not sure why I have to tell you this, but I do."

"Okay," she said and leaned back in one of the living room chairs.

I recounted the first vision I had on the staff outing that showed me Tony sailing, dressed in the dazzling white polo shirt, tan, cargo Bermuda shorts. Cathy started to cry and I was stricken. I started to apologize.

Cathy wiped her eyes and said, "No, you don't understand. There's nothing wrong. Before I closed the casket, I had rolled up his favorite sailing outfit and put it in there. It was a white polo shirt and a pair of tan, cargo shorts. I told him that when he got to the other side he would have his favorite sailing outfit, and he does."

I was unable to move for a few seconds. I didn't know what I was feeling but I continued and told Cathy about seeing Tony with a baby girl and described her in as much detail as I could.

"Oh my God! You couldn't possibly know this but that was our little sister. She was barely a year old when she died. Tony was heartbroken. I'm not sure he ever got over it. He never talked about her again. Now I know he's with her."

I leaned back and felt the couch reach for my back. "Cathy, I didn't know…"

"No. of course not," she said.

"Well, I have just one more incident to tell you about." I told her about visiting Tony's grave and the golden flecks that followed us home.

Cathy took a tissue out of her handbag, dried her eyes and smiled. She looked at me and said, "Okay. Now I have a story for *you*. One of our cousins had a baby some time ago. Tony and I went to visit her and see the baby. Tony held the baby…his eyes were full of tears. Anyway, our cousin wasn't able to come to the funeral, but maybe a week or so after, she called me one morning.

She told me that every morning since the funeral, she'd wake up, look in the mirror, and see little golden flecks on her face. Even when she washed her face, they wouldn't go away. Within an hour or so they disappeared on their own. She concluded it was Tony watching over her." Cathy paused, then looked at me and said, "Janis, I think he's watching over you too."

I didn't know what to think nor what to say. I just sat there hearing in my mind my mother's denigrating tone she used while saying to me. "You were born with a damned veil over your face…" I remembered those snatches of conversations about my great-grandfather and his psychic abilities and everybody down home knew that the last thing in the world you wanted my grandmother to do, especially if you crossed her, was "pray for you!" I remembered my conversation with Kae and as I got older, I did realize that Mama had a gift for praying, healing and manifesting. There was no avoiding or denying these abilities any longer. And I remembered my conversation with Kae. If I needed outside confirmation of having this "gift" Cathy provided that.

Sharing these experiences with her created an instant bond. I told Cathy that I frequently had BMW motorcades driving with me, especially long distances. One weekend on the Taconic Parkway, there was a BMW in front of me, the exact model and color as Tony's. I remembered smiling when I saw it. Then I looked to my left and my right and saw a BMW on each side of me as I approached the rotary. I looked in the rear view mirror and there was another one. A few minutes before I exited from the

Taconic they all vanished literally in the blinking of an eye. I tried not to dwell on it because I knew these incidents would keep happening.

Cathy told me about Tony's "chair." There's a swivel chair in her place that he really liked. Whenever he would come over, he would roll the chair into the kitchen while she cooked. The last time he was there, she never got around to moving the chair back. One evening, a few days after the funeral she was in the kitchen thinking that she really needed to wheel the chair back to the family room. That's when she saw the seat moving from side to side as if Tony was sitting right there slowly swiveling from left to right.

I wanted to tell her that I feel his presence all the time, that he was right here listening to us and that we all needed to rethink exactly what it means to die. It was becoming clearer to me that the average concept of death that so many embraced was wrong. Everlasting life exists. We may not understand how, but it does. I knew it when I was three years old and decades later Tony has confirmed it. What I didn't know then was what else was awaiting me.

I needed to have an intelligent conversation about these so called impossible things especially given the depth of Cathy's loss and this ongoing connection I had with Tony. Cathy could feel Tony's presence also but I knew there was a part of her that viewed the paranormal or psychic elements of my experiences as a little crazy regardless. Right now she was mad at God for taking

Tony but she was certain he was in heaven. Me? I had questions: why did Tony wait twenty years? What happened on his boat? Why did he have to go *now*? What were we supposed to do? Am I supposed to find a way to maintain contact with him, and contribute to the growing knowledge about one's consciousness existing outside of the physical body? For me, God or the Creator or whatever you wanted to call that Force is where our soul resides. We are one small part of that massive, omnipotent consciousness. That's why we have the *potential* to do anything.

Heaven is a journey for me, not an immediate destination upon passing after one lifetime, unless you're an ascended Master, like Christ or Buddha. Heaven is where we evolve to as we get wiser and kinder. Right now I believe *Heaven is a way of being* and it takes a long time to get there. It's something to aspire to over here and over there. To find yourself in Heaven's light, to be among the angels and archangels, to be in the presence of that Force of intelligence and love is the end-game. The wiser and kinder we become the closer we get to that God force. That's a long journey for most of us. It is for me. If there was one thing I was certain of, it was my imperfections! What lies between here and there and all the steps or places in between is extraordinary. Tony's there somewhere. *I just wish I could really see him and touch him. I wish there was a frequency* I could tune into for the best reception and just be with him.

None of us are really alone. I came into this world with that one bit of knowledge. Space is multi-dimensional with many layers to it. I think each layer represents a different vibrational dimension where some kind of intelligent life exists, way beyond the kind you find in a petri dish. Maybe some of us have been programmed or wired from birth to access these different vibrations and see what's going on. Imagine a ream of paper or a very thick book with each page representing a different dimension all coexisting simultaneously. Each one of these pages is a world that exists at its own vibration. The higher the vibration, the more ethereal the existence, the less dense. The lower the vibration, the denser or more solid we are. We're at the low end of the spectrum. The question remains; why some of us can access this now and others can't.

I think human evolution is dependent on whether or not we enable our consciousness to evolve. The universe, where all this is going on, is infinite in size, according to some. There may be multiple universes! Many books with many pages!

There are physicists who say the universe is constantly expanding. From reading, I know there are several highly credentialed scientists discovering formulas and testing theories around psychic phenomena so the western world will feel comfortable accepting what so many indigenous cultures have already known for centuries.

I wanted to tell Cathy, that wherever Tony is, he exists at a higher vibration, so he's more ethereal than we are. Most people don't know how to access that level. For him to be seen with the naked eye by the average person takes an enormous effort on his part. He's crossing dimensions. It's hard. Think of the difficulty astronauts have re-entering the earth's atmosphere.

A good medium can and does bring back messages from the other side. That's not the same as making yourself seen from the other side. I wanted to better understand what's going on right here, in this dimension, and why or how Tony fits into all this.

I also wanted to know what Tony had said to Cathy about me. I wanted every detail. I was also trying to suppress my need for something more from Tony. With each passing day my heart was not only restless but fitful, and my mind was demanding information and understanding as well. I had to find somebody to talk to soon. I thought about all of this on a daily basis.

CHAPTER TWELVE

And Twice On Sundays

I had started attending Tony's church. There was a woman Rector. That alone would've been enough to make me stay, but every time I walked in the sanctuary I felt Tony's presence. The comfort was enormous and it became the setting for several experiences that confirmed for me again that life was everlasting.

No longer did I sit in one of the back pews. As I became more comfortable and secure I moved up and eventually secured "my pew" at the eleven o'clock service on the pulpit side. I had become a familiar face and joined this illustrious church. It was a new community for me and provided a kind of balance that I needed. Never did I expect to feel "at home" in a church, but I did here. There's a definition stating that home is the place you go when you have no other place to go. This church, "our church" was that home for me.

Ten months after Tony died I accepted that his presence was going to be my frequent companion. I had adjusted to his popping up in my meditations and even catching an ethereal glimpse of him. But I didn't know how to explain what happened on Sunday morning while listening to the sermon given by one of the Associate Rectors. It was sunny outside and cast several interesting rays of light through the stained glass windows. I reached for the hymn book, turned my head to the right and saw part of Tony's knee. To be specific, I saw his knee dressed in khaki pants and the lower pocket of a navy blue blazer. It was as if someone had torn the atmosphere and I caught a glimpse of another parallel realm. In seconds, it was gone.

When I got back to my place that afternoon I walked Spike and Yoko wondering how to explain what I had seen. The longer Tony was gone, the more questions I had. I got fixated on what would've happened if he had decided to speak twenty years earlier. I vacillated between sadness and anger. I wasn't longing for some happily ever after ending. It was having the *possibility* taken from me that I found unbearable. Why did he have to go? The more I thought about him drowning the more absurd it became. Something just wasn't right.

I fed the spaniels and fixed dinner for myself. The Sunday Times was waiting for me on the coffee table. I brought my dinner into the living room and sat it down next to the Times. Just as I reached for the remote it happened. I saw a much younger version of myself and Tony in the cabin of his boat. It was smaller than the one he had when he died. He was trying to kiss me while I was unbuttoning his shirt. I heard someone call out to us. I wiggled away from Tony and went up to the deck. The Coast Guard was there.

"A storm's approaching," one of them said. "You should get back to the Marina as quickly as possible. Are you alone?"

Tony walked out and said, "No, I'm her husband. Thanks for letting us know. We'll head in immediately." Satisfied, the Coast Guard left.

"Why did you say you were my husband," I asked, shocked by his audacity.

Tony smiled and said, "Would you *like me to* be your husband?"

I could feel my heart stop for a second. "What? Is this your way of asking me to marry you?"

"Would you like me to be your husband?" he repeated and smiled. "Because I would like you to be my wife."

I stared at him as he slowly walked towards me. I knew he was serious. "Yes, I would love to be your wife," I said never taking my eyes off him.

He kissed and hugged me as tightly as he could.

Then it all vanished. I was back in the living room breathless and overjoyed. Now I knew. That's what would've happened in another timeline, another reality. It wasn't like watching a movie. *I could smell the salt air and feel the dampness as the sky clouded over.* I was wearing one of his white shirts and a pair of jeans. He had on tan Bermuda shorts and a brown plaid shirt with brown buttons. The comfort and resolution that "scene" provided was indescribable. But where did it come from? I had no control over it. If I did, he wouldn't have worn that brown plaid shirt. All I needed was a glimpse to know I hated the shirt!

I thought about writing these scenes down while watching television. The spaniels were sound asleep on the far end of the couch. Taking my empty dinner plate back to the kitchen I admitted to still being tormented by why it took him twenty years to speak. The question would bounce around in my head all night long like one of his basket balls.

A few hours later I put on my pajamas and flopped down in the middle of my bed. I took the remote and turned on the television to watch the news. Yoko was scratching her left ear and Spike was already sleeping.

"Why? Why did it take you so long?" I asked and pulled up a light comforter. "What did you think I would do?"

"Ignore me."

I jumped a little. "Oh my God..." I muttered. Out loud I said, "What woman in her right mind would ignore you?" I groaned and fell back. Thankfully there were several pillows to cushion me. Tomorrow would be here too soon. I turned the t.v. off, the bedside lamp, and forced myself to go to sleep!

The fact that he answered me, with such clarity, I found astounding and joyful. What a relief to know. I wondered what Cathy could tell me.

CHAPTER THIRTEEN

Talking With Cathy

I just knew I was supposed to stay in touch with Cathy. I didn't need anybody to tell me that although Tony did ask. I would've done that anyway. When Cathy lost Tony she lost part of herself. I didn't know how many people around her knew or understood the depth of her loss. Somehow she kept going through the motions. It took persistence to reach Cathy and stay in touch with her. I had to call many times before she responded. Sometimes it would take weeks, sometimes a few months, rarely just a day or two. I couldn't let go because she was my only earthly connection to Tony, to who he was, to what he thought especially about me. I had to stay in touch with Cathy. Eventually she learned I wasn't going to give up, that I would track her down regardless and hang on with the tenacity of a badger. Badger medicine is fierce.

During one visit, she told me she knew who I was because Tony had pointed me out to her several times.

"Really?" I asked.

"Oh yes.'

"But you didn't recognize me at the church," I said.

"Janis, I didn't recognize anybody! I was so out of it, so upset."

"I understand." I remembered the look on her face when I approached her. It was a cross between terror and devastation.

"One evening we saw you walking your dogs and he said to me, 'Look, there she is. What a gorgeous woman.' He was smitten."

"Stop," I said. "He really said I was gorgeous?"

"He did. He really did. Gorgeous and cute. I kept telling him he needed to speak to you. For God's sake, it got to be ridiculous."

"Why didn't he? Twenty-years! I still can't get my head around that!"

"I don't know. Tony would talk to anybody. That's how he perfected his charm. So this didn't make any sense, but I knew something was happening. Tony was a little shy when it came to people who really interested him or impressed him. He said there was just something about you. Every time I told him to speak to you, he'd come up with all kinds of half-baked excuses. Men can be so stupid!"

I sat there and pondered everything she said, but Cathy wasn't finished.

"He thought you were independently wealthy. He told me that. I told him that *he made a good living*. He didn't have anything to be embarrassed by."

I smiled remembering when Tony told me, "They pay me well. I make a good living."

"Janis, he would come by the house sometimes after work and just stand there and … I don't know … talk about you. It was ridiculous! One day I just asked, 'Tony what is it?! Do you want to have sex with this woman, then go do it!'

That statement shocked me. All I could do was stare at Cathy.

She looked at me and said, "He did. He thought you were gorgeous. The two of you had quite a connection," Cathy said.

"Yeah…" I wanted to tell her that we've still got that connection. I wanted to tell her about all the things that were happening. She interrupted my thinking.

"You know, I don't care if the two of you had sex. That's not my concern."

I became motionless. I couldn't recall anyone ever saying something like that to me. I couldn't answer her. I wouldn't answer her. It was a boundary I wasn't going to violate. Some things were still private and I know how that sounds in this world of social media where people reveal everything and anything. That wasn't me. What I wanted to tell her, I sensed she didn't want to hear. I wasn't sure she'd believe me and I needed her to believe me. Tony was "alive" in the afterlife. I thought that was more important than telling her about any sexual encounter between her brother and me.

Cathy invited me to her house for dinner. More pieces of the puzzle fell into place. I walked in and Tony was everywhere, his spirit, his presence, some of his furniture and several of his possessions. I saw that chair he swiveled in after he died. I looked at an unnerving charcoal portrait of him. I walked over to get a closer look and instead saw the two of us in ancient Japan super imposed over the portrait or like a pop-up ad on your computer. We were a couple of some stature during the 1200s. I saw enough to recognize the quality of the robes we were wearing. The image faded.

I walked back in the kitchen where Cathy was preparing dinner and leaned against a counter that was facing the kitchen doorway. It led to the hall and dining room. She was talking and turned around from the sink.

"Janis?" she said. "What are you looking at?"

"Huh? What did you say?"

"*What* are you looking at? Would you like something to drink?"

"When Tony was here did he often stand in the doorway and talk to you?"

She looked at me and then looked at the doorway. "You see Tony don't you?" she asked.

"Yes. He's standing right there," and I pointed. "His left shoulder is leaning against the wall."

On another visit as I was leaving Cathy's house, I saw a black and white photograph that stunned me. I picked it up and asked Cathy why Tony was wearing his hair that way. It was thicker and brushed up on his forehead. It struck me as odd, like a dissonant note in a piano recital.

Cathy said, "Oh, that's not Tony. That's our father."

"My God, they look so much alike." I took a closer look at the woman next to him and realized she looked a little like Tina. I was so unnerved it took me twice as long to drive back to the upper west side from Cathy's house in Park Slope Brooklyn.

I got back to my place and took Spike and Yoko for their last walk of the evening. Traffic had calmed down. Few people were on the street. Three fellow dog walkers were being led by their four leggeds. Yoko and Spike stopped to sniff a lamppost while I worried about Cathy. Her grief was palpable. Sometimes I thought our grief represented opposite sides of the same coin. I didn't know how to help her. All I could do was listen and that felt inadequate. The common ground we shared was Tony. We weren't going to "hang out." I was sure her idea of fun was my idea of misery and vice versa. The fabric of our lives was different. I hoped that we could be there for each other in some way, check in from time to time. That would have to be enough.

Tony's death, the way he died, Cathy's grief, my experiences were converging, forming some new configuration that was transforming me in a way I couldn't articulate. I could feel it but I couldn't speak it.

CHAPTER FOURTEEN

Meanwhile

2009-2010

You know that expression? When it rains it pours? A monsoon enveloped my life. Friends continued to die and I was becoming a professional eulogizer. Giving one for my friend, Claire, who was the epitome of style and grace, as I walked up to the pulpit to speak weariness took over. In a flash I understood a small bit of what Ted Kennedy, U.S. Senator from Massachusetts, had to feel eulogizing so many in his family who had died in very public ways. After the service and reception I went back to Claire's home where a few of the adults had gathered while the "young people" went out. I was reintroduced to her sister, Anne. We hit it off in that mysterious way when you click with someone. I didn't know it then but we would end up saving each other's lives.

It was a little over two years since Tony drowned. The grief was still fresh. The ache was persistent. And the economy tanking due to the housing crisis indirectly resulted in me losing two thirds of my income. I couldn't afford to stay in the city any longer although I tried to find ways to make ends meet. The harder I tried the worse it became. I was beginning to feel out flanked.

I was walking to Zabar's, pondering the ugly reality that had arrived. I hoped that some Nova lox would help soothe my worries. Waiting for the light to change so I could cross Broadway, I noticed there was a woman standing next to me. I found myself thinking about Tony and what life would've been like if he had lived. Something made me turn and I saw a woman looking at me. It wasn't a hostile glare. It was a gentle gaze with a warm smile. My immediate thought was she couldn't be a native New Yorker. You don't look at anybody on the street! But I knew this woman from somewhere. Her white hair was neatly pulled back into a bun. She had a dark green light weight coat perfect for early fall. Her sparkling grey eyes were exceptional. They were so clear you could see your reflection and then I remembered. This was the woman I saw at Tony's funeral. She knew Tony was standing next to me. The light changed and we both just stood there looking at each other.

"I know you," I said. "You attended Tony Carter's funeral. That was almost two years ago." People were walking around us in that brusque way New Yorkers have so we stepped to the side.

"Yes," she said. "Can we go somewhere and talk?"

"Umm, I was going to Zabar's. I don't live too far from here." I thought for a few seconds. "I'm going to take a chance here. Would you like to come back to my place?"

She smiled and said, "If that's what you'd like to do, fine. Stop worrying. I'm not going to harm you. Why don't we do this? You go to Zabar's. I have an errand or two and I'll meet you back at your place."

"Great," I said. "It shouldn't take me more than twenty minutes or so. Is there anything I can get you at Zabar's? Some Babka? It's really wonderful."

She smiled and said, "No. I'm fine."

I hurried across the street and remembered I hadn't told her my address. I went back to find her and she'd gone. I didn't see her anywhere. I sensed that I was about to have a significant experience, something that I'd never gone through before. I ran over to Zabar's, saw Wally, picked up a few things and rushed back. Just as I turned the corner of 81st Street and West End Avenue, I saw her standing in front of my building. We looked at each other for a second or two.

"Who are you?" I asked knowing she couldn't or wouldn't tell me.

"Let's say Tony sent me. Can we go inside?"

"Of course," I said. As we walked through the lobby, I studied this woman. I didn't believe she was real. She wasn't a hallucination. She looked very solid, but everything in me screamed she wasn't of this realm. I wished my grandmother was here. "What's your name?"

"Galen." The elevator came and we rode up to my floor.

"I have these cocker spaniels. They can be a little overwhelming," I said.

"I know. Don't worry about it," she said. "I love dogs."

We walked in and Yoko and Spike rushed towards me, saw Galen and barked. She bent down to pet them and they calmed down. I showed her into the living room. She looked around and said, "This is a lovely place. So many books; the art work is wonderful."

"Thank-you. Can I get you something? Tea? Wine? I don't drink coffee."

"Whatever you're having will be fine with me," she said.

"Okay, give me a minute and I'll be right back." Spike and Yoko were watching her. I fixed a pot of tea, cut a few slices of the chocolate babka I'd bought and looked for a tray to put all of this on including sugar, tea cups and spoons. I sat everything down on the coffee table and waited.

Galen poured herself a cup of tea, put two spoonfuls of sugar, gently stirred it and took a sip. "This is lovely," she said. I noticed her skin was flawless, velvet like and seemed to glow. She could have been forty or eighty. Galen looked timeless.

"Galen, "I said, "You need to tell me something."

"I know that you're struggling with Tony's departure, as is his sister, Cathy. But you are so *unresolved, searching, wondering* about the sequence of events, what you've experienced." Galen paused. For a minute I sensed she was listening to something or someone else for instructions. She continued and said, "We decided to find you after Tony contacted us."

I wanted to ask her how she knew, and how Tony sent her, who or what is 'we' and that voice said to me, "Shut up and listen."

"There has been a great deal of legitimate study done on the afterlife. No one leaves here before they're supposed to, even if it's an accident. Under the right conditions, there are people who can serve as conduits to manifest the dead."

"What do you mean by *manifest*?" I asked.

"Well, there's a range... Some can enable those who have passed over to come back through their voices. Right now you hear Tony inside your head for the most part. There have been a few times when you have heard him as if he were standing next to you. You're blessed. Then there are others who become a vehicle for those who've passed over to actually come back into this dimension. It's risky for the person who is the conduit." She sighed and then said, "Of course, there are exceptions to all of this when they manage to appear with no help, no conduit. It's a huge effort for them to do that."

I sat there, gleeful and stunned. "Who are these people who can do that? Bring them back?" I asked and took note of what was happening in the living room. The atmosphere had changed. It seemed to glow and vibrate. It was subtle but significant.

"These are special mediums, physical mediums, different from mediums who convey messages with specific information. Legitimate ones have information so specific there's no way they could make it up or read about it somewhere. Physical mediums are in a class by themselves. Under the right conditions these are the people who can serve as a conduit to manifest the voices of the dead. *Their voice comes through the medium*. There are other cases where those who have passed over come back for a very short amount of time. There are records of this in your world." Galen picked up a piece of Babka, and looked at it as if she didn't know what to do with it.

"I need to read something. I need information," I said. Frustrated, I stared off into space thinking about how to better articulate what I needed. "I guess I need somebody to confirm at least some of what I've experienced...I need to know what is happening. No. I need to know if there's anybody else out there who understands the scope of this, who can help me verify this in some way."

"Tony's driving this, you know." Galen had managed to pick up the slice of babka, break off a piece and place it with great care in her mouth.

I nodded my head and watched a smile spread across her face as she chewed the babka. I was fascinated by her and sensed this was the first time she had ever chewed anything! Any moment Tony might show up. At least I really thought that and actually looked over to the Eames chair. Spike and Yoko were lying on the couch observing Galen with an unusual calmness.

"I so need him. It's the magnitude of all this, Galen. My sightings, his ongoing existence and where he is. What is it I'm seeing? This gift has been with me all my life, but never like this. *Never this dramatic.* I've walked down the street seeing things and people nobody else is seeing. I walk into a room full of people and my head gets crammed with all kinds of information about them, about what they're feeling, what they've been through. I have a conversation with someone and what they say is only half the information I get about them and I've learned what not to say all these years. You don't tell everything you know. But this? This is something else and I've got to get more information. It's got to be out there." I covered my eyes for a minute and shook my head from side to side. "Tony's here. I can feel him."

Galen laughed. "He's here whenever you need him."

I looked at her and said, "I've *felt* Tony. *I've felt his presence, his body but it wasn't solid, flesh and blood.* But he's gone ... He wasn't a perfect man but I knew he would be perfect for me. I need information."

"Of course and there *is* information on the afterlife, on physical mediumship, on all of it. You also need a community of people like yourself, Janis, like your real self. It's time."

"Galen, tell me who has come back from the dead? Let me rephrase that. How does one cross the dimension of the afterlife to come back here to this realm? *Who has done that* because when I see them they are still very much over there, ethereal. Only Tony has been back in a way that I could feel."

"Your grandparents have been back. But I understand what you mean about Tony and the experiences you've had," Galen said.

"Has anyone come back in a material form or body for any length of measureable time? Ten minutes or ten days! Who has done that? And who has witnessed it?"

"Jesus Christ did," Galen said very matter of factly.

That stopped me. I sat and thought for a minute or two and then said, "I believe that without any doubt. That's why Easter is my favorite holiday. It recognizes and celebrates eternal life."

Galen's face was beaming.

"I know what the Bible says, that He died, was resurrected and stayed here on earth for forty days before he ascended. That in Corinthians it says He appeared to more than 500 people after he died and his Disciples saw him at least four times after he died. I got that! But, with all due respect, most people need more than the Bible. I know that sounds so awful but there are people out there who are never going to believe this without some form of 'evidence,' or something they can hang onto in their world, and not feel stupid or gullible. And a lot of them are Christians or people of faith."

"You'd be surprised how many answers are in the Bible and other holy books here on earth," Galen said motionless. I wasn't sure she had moved her mouth.

"The people I'm talking about are right outside this door. Some of them are people of faith, some of them aren't, but all of them revel in their intelligence. My grandmother would call many of them educated fools. If they can't see or touch it, it doesn't exist. There's got to be additional information. The people who want to believe but don't dare to, I care about them," I said. I got up, walked over to the window and sat back down. "I reach a lot of them when I do my show. They consider themselves well-informed and logical, but they don't want to look like fools. They want to understand. How do I make the incomprehensible less daunting? Who or what I am is not enough."

"I understand. What you need to do is start looking. The work is out there. You're very good at tracking down information and people. You already have one friend who's looking into matters related to all of this and more."

"I'm not interested in 'converting' anybody. But I despise stupidity and what I call deliberate ignorance."

Right then, I heard Tony say, "I told you, intelligent. You are so intelligent."

"I agree with Tony. You are intelligent." Galen smiled and I had to confront that I was having a conversation with someone out of the ordinary in every sense. The room was electric. That vibration I noticed earlier had become a soft hum and the spaniels seemed to still be unusually calm, at peace.

The living room felt as if it and all that was in it had been temporarily suspended along with the rules that governed physics. I did feel like time had stopped, like we were in some sort of bubble or another world sealed off from the activities going on outside of my living room.

I sighed heavily, leaned back and carefully observed Galen. I wondered if Galen was really her name. For the next few seconds we watched each other. I didn't feel threatened or in danger. The word or expression, other worldly, came to mind. She did more than look into my eyes. She went into them! Her gaze consumed me and I sensed that she knew all of my secrets, hopes, fears, ambitions, desires, mistakes and pain. I was naked. The tables were turned on me.

I sat up, looked her straight in the eye and heard myself say, "Okay, I'm ready. Tell me what I have to do."

Galen laughed. The sound of her voice reminded me of bells or wind chimes. She poured herself another cup of tea.

"You really believe that had Tony lived the two of you would've married?"

I was taken aback by her question and wondered where she was going. "Well, I think…no I feel it, deeply.

"I believe you're right, but you and Tony are still together, even with the veil between you *because you can see through it.* You have to decide how much of a relationship you want with him. Both of you have work to do over here and over there. You might end up with what a friend of yours called a cosmic marriage."

I was barely breathing. I wondered how she knew about this particular friend of mine but deep down I did know. "So what do I do?" I asked.

"Do what you do best, read, think, write, communicate." She finished her second cup of tea and said, "I have to go now. I'm so glad we ran into each other." Galen stood up and looked around. "You'll be leaving this place. Your time here is finished you know."

I knew she was right but I didn't want to admit it yet and I couldn't handle knowing how she knew at this moment. I walked her to the door and asked, "Will I see you again?"

She turned towards me and said, "I doubt it. You won't need to see me again."

I put my hand on the door knob and said, "If I were to ask you where you lived, would you tell me?"

"No," she said and smiled.

"I didn't think so," I said.

Looking into my eyes she said, "You know where I live."

"How do I thank you?" I wanted to reach for her hand but didn't. I was a little afraid.

She laughed and said, "Read, think, write, communicate in that order. You have work to do. Tony will help." She touched the side of my face for a split second and left.

I locked the door overwhelmed by the touch of her hand that felt like a combination of velvet and leather. I turned, leaned against the door, and slid an inch at a time to the floor. I sat there, elbows on my knees, my head in my hands and eyes closed. Yoko and Spike trotted over to me and Yoko started to lick my face. Within seconds the atmosphere changed. Something shifted and everything felt normal. Sitting on the floor I realized I had to go to the station tomorrow. Who knew what fresh hell awaited me there. I looked at the spaniels and realized I needed to take them out. I was drained and there was nobody to talk to about this except for Kae.

CHAPTER FIFTEEN

Cataclysmic Upheavals

It took me several days to digest Galen's visit while going through the motions of daily life. When I told Kae that I ran into Galen on the corner of Broadway and 81st Street, her initial fear was for my safety. Then I filled in the blanks. Kae was unusually quiet when I finished.

"Lord have mercy, Janis," was the first thing she said. "I think you had some kind of visitation."

"Yeah," I said. "Now what?"

"You need to remember everything she said."

And I tried. I even wrote down what I remembered only to have it vanish.

During the next five months my life plunged into an uncontrollable state. The life I had been living for decades was being undone. No matter what I did, I couldn't rescue myself, and I tried. If my life were a chess game, other people or forces were making the moves. I was just another pawn in a game I hadn't figured out yet.

Galen's visit stayed with me. I took her advice and started to read, think and write.

Through it all, Tony remained in the forefront of my thoughts. I kept wondering about "what if," and if there were parallel or alternative lifetimes being played out in some dimension regarding what happened to us? What were we doing?

Where did we live? Did we have children? These were questions that had become a second skin to me while I went through each day becoming more and more concerned about how I was going to continue living in the city minus two thirds of my income especially if I could no longer do my radio show. I wasn't making a ton of money but it was enough to make living in the city feasible. The country remained my salvation, my refuge.

Lucinda called one evening and asked if she could come over while I was out there for a few days. I said, "Of course." A half-hour later she arrived with her husband, Theo. This couldn't be good. We went in the living room and sat down. I asked if I could get them anything, tea, wine, water. Lucinda shook her head and motioned for me to sit down. Her husband, Theo, had a meek smile on his face.

"Miss Janis, Theo and I have come to a decision."

"What kind of decision, Lucinda? What's going on?" I asked.

Lucinda sighed and said, "We are going back to Nicaragua."

I kept my mouth closed and looked first at Lucinda and then Theo before asking, "Why? What happened?"

"You know we've been here a long time, Miss Janis. We're grateful for what this country did for us. You helped us get citizenship. We work hard. We save our money. Our children are almost on their own…"

Theo cleared his throat, sat up straight and said, "Life here is getting too difficult, too mean. My son goes to the city, gets stopped for no reason other than being Latino. We make sure he's dressed nice, neat. I know you understand. He's going to graduate in December and he can make his own decision. He'll be 22. Our daughter already found a good job here. She's going to stay. But we're hoping our son will come home too. There's a role for him there. Here? Too hateful. Too mean. Every time he leaves the house, goes into Manhattan, I wonder if that's the last time I'll see him."

"We want to go home. Things aren't what they used to be in Nicaragua when I had to leave. We have family there, some land."

"I don't know what to say. I want you to be happy, to feel safe. If you'll be happy and feel safe in Nicaragua – so be it. When do you want to leave?" I asked.

"Right after our son graduates," Lucinda said.

I just sat there, stiff with grief and panic. I wanted to scream and tell them, "You can't go. You're part of my life. Please, don't go." I didn't say that. Instead, I took a deep breath and said, "How can I help you make this transition? Is there anything I can do?"

As we talked for the next hour, somewhere during the pauses and memories we shared, I decided to sell the country place. As much as I loved the house there were some problems. This was a community that didn't embrace diversity of any sort. I knew people put garbage in the driveway. I'd often clean it up before Lucinda got to work, but she knew. I sensed that this was as far as the "neighbors" would go, but why push it? I could always build another house.

Lucinda and Theo got up and Lucinda asked, "What are you going to do, Miss Janis?"

"Well, it may be time for me to go also."

She grabbed my hand and squeezed it hard. "I don't want anything to happen to you."

"I am going to be fine. When I was much younger, I had an accountant who said I always managed to land on my feet. I'll be fine." I let them out and watched them drive away. I did not believe I was going to be fine. I sensed this was the beginning of the end. What I didn't know was the end of what.

I walked back into the living room and said out loud, "So, Tony, what's up? You need to tell me if you know." No response. No presence. I threw my hands up in the air in exasperation. I thought about calling Kae but she hadn't been feeling well lately and it troubled me. I often forgot that Kae was approaching her eightieth birthday. So I sat down, opened my lap top and started researching realtors. By the end of the week, I had put the house on the market. It took some doing to sell it for reasons I don't understand. When a buyer was found, I sold it at a loss. I walked away with money but I lost a substantial amount also. I put that money in the bank and hoped it might tide me over in the city until something else came along, or I invented something to do that would earn me some more money. But the harder I tried, the worse it became.

I held onto the radio job and then that imploded. I didn't get fired. They simply asked me to do something I thought was stupid. My own "brand" did not include stupid. How do you make a conscious decision to demean your reputation? I resigned. The decision to leave the city was made for me. You need money to live in New York and a lot of it. This was becoming the reality for most major cities on the Atlantic seacoast, Boston, Philadelphia, Baltimore, Washington, D.C. But New York City, especially Manhattan and now Brooklyn, was in a class by itself. I just didn't know where to go. The house money provided a cushion, but it wouldn't last long in Manhattan.

During all this, Galen's visit was still on my mind. It had been a little less than a month since we had our talk in my living room. I started looking for information on the after life. I was amazed at what I found regarding that and related subjects, like near death experiences, research into the ongoing existence of one's consciousness after bodily death, investigations by Nobel Price winning scientists on ectoplasm and its connection to manifesting the dead, and spiritualism. There were astrophysicists studying psychic phenomena, along with black holes, worm holes, time travel, the "size" of the universe, the possibilities of parallel time lines and on and on.

I spent one Saturday immersed in this information, leaving only to walk Spike and Yoko. Our last walk of the day took me by

Tony's building and I realized I had not talked with Christine in almost a month. I had not told her about Galen because I didn't want to listen to her skepticism and doubt, and I didn't want to feel her fear. It made me angry.

We finished our last walk around 10:00 PM. I decided to fix myself something to eat. I had forgotten supper although I had fed Spike and Yoko! My mind wandered through possibilities. Every now and then I let myself ask, what would our wedding have been like? How big? And the dress? Sighing, I scoped out the contents of the refrigerator and found something to eat, cold salmon, couscous, and the makings of a good salad. I reached for a bottle of Coke, opened it and began slicing some cherry tomatoes for the salad. I turned the radio on and heard the last few bars of "...gonna' be all right, all right..." Hmph, I mumbled. Spike and Yoko were lying in the kitchen doorway hoping some food would magically jump off the counter and into their mouths!

Everything was not all right. I put my dinner on a tray and walked into the living room, turned on the television and proceeded to watch the eleven o'clock news. Something seemed to shift in the air, and for a moment I thought Tony was in the room. I finished eating, cleaned up, and the spaniels and I went to our bedroom. As I got ready for bed I continued to think about the wedding that never was. I crawled in bed, reached for a magazine, fell back on the pillows and heard, "This is what happened."

It was like watching a movie trailer. I saw our wedding, or at least snatches of it. I saw myself putting on my wedding dress, pink skirt with delicate white embroidered flowers forming the bodice. The embroidered flowers were "scattered" below the waist, and I had on pink satin flats, a fashion irregularity. There were no bridesmaids, no flower girls. I saw myself panic and ask the friend who was going to walk me down the aisle to go to the sanctuary and make sure Tony really wanted to go through with this! When we did walk down the aisle my friend was cracking jokes under his breath to calm me down. I was nervous. Candles lit every pew. I saw myself at the altar and Tony grabbing my hand and smiling. And that was it. It all faded. I didn't. I sat in bed and played that scene over and over. I cherished it. A year or so later, I found "my" wedding dress on Pinterest, the exact one I had seen in…what? A vision? A glimpse into another universe, a parallel universe? I didn't know and I didn't care but I was fascinated.

Where did that scene come from? I found no answers that night. One thing was certain. It wasn't my imagination. When I used my imagination, I created everything. I was in charge. What I just watched was out of my control. I tried to change what I saw; change the wedding gown, change the church, eliminate the candles, come up with a whole new scenario. I could no more do that than I could change the content of something being televised or witnessed from afar. This was only the first glimpse of an alternative or parallel reality I was allowed to see over the following weeks and months.

What happened shortly before I left the station was related to this. I was walking back from picking up lunch at a nearby Deli. I turned the corner and found myself on the campus of Yale University! Our son was graduating and Tony was beside me with our daughter in front of us. Somehow I knew my son's name was Zachary. He was tall like his father and was walking slightly ahead of us. Meredith, our daughter was seven years younger than Zachary. The excitement was visceral, proud parents, relieved students, and faculty members feeling vindicated! The weather was beautiful, clear skies, warm breeze and the campus bursting with the green glow of spring grass and plants... and then it was gone. I was back in Manhattan walking into the station with a pastrami on rye with brown mustard and two pickles.

I had all of my things from the country put in storage until I came up with a plan. Every logical step I took to cut back on expenses over the remaining months backfired. Just before leaving my place on West End Avenue, Yoko passed away. She was 18. I was heartbroken but grateful to have had her for so long. Spike and I continued with me finding time to look for another spaniel. This time I would adopt.

Moving to a smaller place in the city did not save me money. Borrowing money did not help and there were no jobs for the *"over qualified."* There were many friends who lent a helping hand during this time, but it didn't matter. The money monsters kept trying to choke the life out of me. I gave in to what I had been sensing for some time. I stopped fighting and accepted that something or someone was pushing me out of New York City. Finally I put my things from the city in storage and became technically homeless. Spike and I stayed with friends after leaving the neighborhood that had become my adult home, and aside from the country, the only home Spike and Yoko knew. It felt like my life was being dismantled at best, at worst demolished with a wrecking ball! There was nothing subtle about any of this. The only thing that kept me grounded was Tony's church. He left me in good hands. That and the fact that deep down I knew I had accepted being pushed out of New York. I was relieved.

Shortly after spending Thanksgiving with some friends who lived just outside of the city, I called Anne. We had kept in touch sporadically since her sister's death. Anne had moved earlier that year to a winter wonderland in northern New England. I told her what a mess things were and that it was difficult for Spike and me to be in other people's homes no matter how gracious they were. Dog people were a specific type and I had found a Cavalier Spaniel to adopt. She was being delivered within days. Anne invited me to come up north, stay a few weeks, and sort out what I wanted to do. Spike would be no problem. She had three dogs and a cat. One or two more wouldn't matter! I agreed to come up with Spike and the new Cavalier. Five dogs, one cat and two humans... I thought, this ought to be interesting. I thanked my hosts and left. I didn't say goodbye to anyone else. I just vanished. The only people I stayed connected to were those at the big, fancy church. They became my anchor. Somehow I would find a way to stay connected.

I stopped at the appointed location to pick up my adopted Cavalier Spaniel. Her name was Amber and I'm convinced she's an angel. She jumped in the car with Spike in the back seat. He was very curious about this new addition to the family and literally sniffed her out. She sat in the passenger seat as I locked the car doors and fastened my seat belt. The directions to the far north were taped to my dashboard. Spike had settled down and Amber crawled into my lap. A five to six hour drive awaited, depending on traffic and weather. It was December and snow was a possibility. I started the car and pulled out onto the highway leaving behind a life that was finished. I had no idea what awaited me. All I did know, was that after driving for a little over an hour, I glanced at the passenger seat and caught a glimpse of Tony. I heard him say, "Everything's going to be all right." I wished I knew what all right meant.

PART TWO

...and what was meant to be...

CHAPTER SIXTEEN

I Could Breathe

December 2010

It was a miracle that I found Anne's place. You really had to be looking for it. The house sat on a private road with only two others. Each house sat on two to four acres. Anne's house was a deceptive looking structure. From the outside it looked small. Once you got inside a different truth presented itself.

We pulled into her driveway that gently sloped downward. You could either go forward to the front door or bear right down to the garage. I remember pulling into the driveway and stopping so I could get a partial view of the backyard and the view that spread out beyond it. It was a heavily wooded area. Beyond that I saw sky and mountains, not a building or skyscraper in sight. It was wonderful! As I stopped the car Spike woke up. Amber repositioned herself in the passenger seat as I unlocked the car door and stepped out. I was stiff and fatigued from the drive. My neck and shoulder muscles were tight with pain and I was hungry.

The minute I stepped from the car, it was as if someone waved a magic wand from my head to my feet. Every ounce of tension melted away. A clean, cold breeze flowed by and left me with a baptismal sensation. I was startled by it and half expected someone to walk out from the woods to welcome me! For the first time in years, I felt like I could breathe. The air was clean and fresh and cold. Some of the trees looked like blue spruce. They were dark green, thick, and you could smell their presence in the air. Maple and birch trees populated the yard. I had a sneaky suspicion that we were very close to Canada. Was it ever really warm in Canada? I didn't think so. I was still looking around, tilted my head back and looked up. There was nothing but an unobstructed view of the sky. I got back in the car and pulled up to the front door that was painted bright red. Always a good sign I thought. Red was one of my favorite colors. The three of us got out. Spike and Amber relieved themselves on the winter lawn. The front yard was bordered by more trees. You could barely see through them to the road. There was another house on the other side and another at the end of the road. That was it. That was the "neighborhood." We turned and walked up the front steps. The house was painted light grey with white trim. Anne opened the front door to my new life.

Spike, Amber and I were greeted by Sawyer, an English Cocker Spaniel who formerly belonged to Claire, Anne's sister, McKenzie, an elderly Golden Retriever, Brandy, an elegant older lady, a mixed breed, and eventually Jesse, who had to be one of the oldest cats in the world! He moved at his own pace and to hell with everybody else. There was some barking and a lot of sniffing of rear ends among the four leggeds. This was going to be interesting, I thought. How much of an adjustment would this be and for whom?

There was a door that separated the foyer from the living room, but the door had glass panes allowing you to see into the living room. The far wall was mostly glass. But it was almost dark and I couldn't see what the view was.

Anne showed us around and I was surprised at how much space the house actually had. The living room floor with a wood burning fireplace was really the middle level. The kitchen, dining area, powder room, Anne's suite with her own bath, a powder room, and the sunroom (that was originally the dining room) made up the middle or entry level. Upstairs was a loft area that was almost half the size of the living and dining areas. Downstairs were two bedrooms, a living room area with a wood stove and full bath. There was also the door to the garage, and a sliding glass door to the backyard. Anne had prepared one of those bedrooms for us.

I unloaded the car, fed Spike and Amber. I always needed to unwind after driving and that was a slow process. It was similar to coming out of a coma. Lucinda understood but she wasn't here. A friend said, I was always a very focused driver, a by product of learning to drive in New York City! I'm sure Anne and I ate, and I'm sure we talked. What I remember is Spike, Amber and me getting into an unfamiliar bed and falling asleep. I was too tired to think about anything.

The next morning, I got dressed and the three of us walked up the stairs. As I got to the top, I turned right to see the view and felt the power of the location. The view was breath taking, from left to right nothing but mountains, trees and sky with an occasional hawk flying by. At this time of the year, snow covered the mountain tops. This panoramic view would cure whatever ailed you.

I don't know how long I stood there looking but Spike made it clear it was time to go out. Anne left for work before I got up and had confined her pets to her bedroom. I felt badly about that. I hoped she wasn't doing that because of Spike, Amber and me. I made a mental note to ask her.

Spike, Amber and I went for a walk around this new place. We strolled down the private road that had virtually no traffic, and understood that it was possible for a deer or a moose to come sauntering out from the woods to cross our path. This was different! For a moment I thought about my grandfather and how he would've loved this place as long as we could keep warm! That superseded fashion. Tina would've been horrified. Mama would be concerned that I'd catch pneumonia and Tony? "Let's stay inside. It's too cold out here." I smiled remembering that he told me one winter day that he thought he was allergic to the cold. We would've stayed inside.

Amber, Spike and I all turned around to walk back to the house. I was looking at the road, the bare birch trees, a few orphaned leaves left to converse with winter, plant life that had succumbed to the cold until spring. Amber seemed to be doing just fine. Spike trotted along eagerly smelling and marking everything. They both had on winter coats and looked more comfortable than I felt. The temperature had to be in the single digits. We turned to walk down the driveway to the house, and there was Tony, standing at the door as if he were waiting for us to return. I could feel him smile. I was overjoyed, and then he was gone, but I knew he would be back.

CHAPTER SEVENTEEN

Losses

2011-2012

As the days went by, I finally admitted how weary I was. Often I'd just get up, walk Amber and Spike, fix breakfast for all of us, make sure Anne's creatures were settled, and then sink into the couch and look at the view. I convinced Anne to let Brandy, Sawyer and Kenzie out of her bedroom and roam the house since I was there. Looking out the glass doors, I tried to draw strength from the mountains and keep my eye on Spike.

Two weeks before we left, an emergency trip to the Animal Hospital in Manhattan revealed Spike had advanced cancer. The attending vet said I should put him down right then. The way the vet delivered the news showed little to no empathy. I wondered if she would agree to have someone she loved put down immediately upon hearing a terminal diagnosis. I looked at her and said, "I can't do that right now." What I wanted to do was slap her into next year. She looked slightly disgusted and told me Spike could be in pain. I told her to give me some pain killers, which she did, and we left. I had one eye on the mountain and another on Spike. A week after we arrived, Spike passed away late one evening on the couch. I knew it was coming but it didn't minimize the pain or grief. Amber, Spike and I spent the rest of the night on the couch. I was a wreck and fell asleep crying. It was almost as if Spike lived just long enough to give Amber instructions on how to handle me and what to expect. A few days after Yoko passed she came back to me one day and licked my face, telling me all was well. Maybe Spike would let me know. Morning arrived and Anne drove me to a local vet where they handled Spike's cremation. Riding back to the house with Amber in my lap, I wondered, what next?

What followed was a maelstrom of change. Thankfully, Amber, Sawyer, 'Kenzie, and Brandy prevented me from dwelling on Spike's loss but not quite. To this day I miss and think about him as I do all my other spaniels that have graced my life. The week following Spike's loss, I was sitting on the couch staring at the mountains when I came to the conclusion that I couldn't stay here forever and I certainly couldn't stay much longer without paying Anne something. But then what? Where would I go?

I now owned my childhood home down south that my grandfather built. I could always go home. It survived Katrina. Our house was the only house left intact on the block. I remember the night Katrina hit, lying awake worrying about the house and the survival of some cousins I grew up with, one of whom was living in the house with his family. They stayed there during the storm. Every time I'd think about the house during Katrina's onslaught, I would see an image of it with Papa standing next to it on one side and Mama on the other. They looked very calm, serene. The storm didn't seem to bother them. They were also the size of Egyptian gods standing outside of their temples or palaces. I know my grandparents protected that house. Theoretically, it shouldn't have survived. It should've been torn apart like so many other houses on the block. The houses I came to know as a child were either gone or severely damaged. The surrounding area resembled a war zone and it was never completely restored. I didn't know if I could handle seeing that.

Shortly after Tina died, I had the house gutted, updated and renovated. It was a sturdy house that Tina almost wrecked with her "renovations" that *excluded* rewiring but included the addition of a back porch that she refused to let the contractor properly build, and enclosing the front porch that prevented air from circulating throughout the house and keeping it cool during the summer. The second bathroom she added included fake wood walls and flooring that had buckled. Somehow she managed to spend a lot of money and devalue the house with her decisions.

A friend from Tony's church said that if I went back there to live, I'd be killed in two weeks! That might have been a slight exaggeration, but not by much. The minute I opened my mouth and started talking, they would know. I'd go home and be a stranger, perceived as a serious threat to the order and rule of things. Black folks still vanished in Mississippi, still got harassed, still were targeted as "problems." Things were getting worse for black people everywhere in different, equally dangerous ways in the 21st century just as they had been before the Civil Rights Movement. One thing about black folks from Mississippi, we know how to survive. Although my heart still wanted to go home, my head put an end to that idea. Survival exacts a huge price in those circumstances.

So here I was in northern New Hampshire, a part of the country I *never* dreamed about nor had any desire to even visit unless I had to. Campaign workers for the Jesse Jackson Presidential run of 1984 referred to New Hampshire as "up south Alabama." This was the moment when I felt like I had been picked up by the scruff of my neck and plopped down in this remote part of the country. For what? And by whom?

Anne asked if I would consider staying and splitting the expenses. I understood residential real estate only in the context of New York City where space was as precious as gold and equally as costly. An entire apartment could fit on the entry floor of this house, and be considered a luxury property! If you knocked down all of the walls you'd had an enviable (small) loft space worthy of TriBeCa or Soho. How much was this going to cost me? I was afraid of what she would tell me. When she did, I was shocked. It was pittance compared to the expenses I had in the city. I would be stupid to turn this down so I didn't! Anne was delighted to get someone to share expenses with, *and* I was a dog lover and Amber was very comfortable, so all was well! But it was more than economics and a love of four legged creatures. Although I had not known Anne for very long, there were moments when I felt we could read each other's minds! There was an uncanny familiarity Anne and I shared punctuated by often saying the same thing at the same time, finishing each other's sentences and sharing a history with money tangled up by a parent or parents who were forty bricks short of a full load.

We also shared some radical differences. She loved the cold. I loved the heat. She didn't really care about fashion. I found that incomprehensible! She was pennywise and pound foolish. Pennies didn't go very far in my world. I was always focused on bigger pictures, bigger plans that generated serious money. Anne was striving to lead a life of simplicity. She tossed out things with frightening ease. There was nothing simple about my life and I loved acquiring beautiful things. She was oddly inconsistent while my sanity was held together by routine. Organized religion left her cold while spirituality was my safety net and organized religion served a necessary purpose in this insane world. I talked to the dead and often my work demanded I talk to a wide range of people! She barely wanted to talk with the living but had shared spaces in the past with others, and had been married and divorced. I lived alone all my adult life and had never married. She had three siblings. I had none. We were opposite sides of the same coin.

I was standing behind the couch one day, looking at the view after having been there a little over a month, and told Anne that this was a clean space. I wasn't referring to dust or grim. I was referring to the spirit and energy of the place. I didn't know what Anne thought at the time, but she didn't wince or run out of the house. I wasn't ready to tell her about anything else…yet.

I can't remember exactly when I told her about Tony, but I remember the look on her face. It was deliberately blank. She was trying to show no reaction. His death was sad and she said the right things. The visions? She tried to look unalarmed but she was intrigued. Seeing the dead? Most people think you're crazy but when you start to describe someone you've never seen that's recognized by another person... things change. I did that once. Afterwards, I received the kind of respect that's driven by fear.

Several months later I had the movers bring most of my furniture. Amber and I would have the entire lower floor. I squeezed in as many of my things as I could without creating an environment that would drive me crazy. There were many things that had to stay in storage. Boxes of unpacked books, dishes and art supplies found a home in the garage and I hated it! Retrieving my plants was a separate project. It was essential to my well being that I have them, along with my books and art work. Anne was stunned by the size and health of these plants. Two were classified as heirloom because of their age.

I kept Kae informed. She grudgingly approved, a little suspicious of Anne. During our conversations Kae started to make comments about her health. Something was wrong. The more she talked about these symptoms, the more afraid for her I became. She went to the doctor and after complaining about the care she received, she let on that her condition was serious. It was hard to get any specific information from her, her husband or her daughter. I knew Kae was dying long before it became obvious. The last time she was hospitalized, we talked. Her voice was barely above a whisper. After hanging up, I knew I would never hear her voice in this world again.

Her daughter, Janice, called a few days later and said, "Mother's passed."

"No, no, no…" I said. "Don't tell me this." Who would I talk with now?

"Baby I know, but she's gone," Janice said.

I didn't have to pretend to be anything other than what I was with Kae. All of me was acceptable to Kae especially the Southern part. Losing her left a hole too big for anyone to fill. I felt like all the air raced out of me when she died. Another loss. From time to time I imagined Kae meeting Tony on the other side. I could see the smile on her face and the glint in her eyes as she approached "Sailor Man." I imagined Kae walking right up to him and holding his hand in both of hers, thrilled to meet him, and then asking, "Why did you leave so soon?"

Tony was around. He was drifting in and out of my new residence. It was as if he became part of the air I breathed until I went downstairs. Once my furniture arrived, it felt like he moved in too! I sensed that he approved of the new surroundings but I didn't know why. The last thing I sensed on many nights before falling asleep was Tony.

It took me awhile to adjust to living in a place with a population of roughly nine hundred people and few if any sidewalks. You drove everywhere. Winter was beautiful due to the snow. I loved it so long as I didn't have to go outside. Winter transformed into some version of mud season for a few weeks and then one day it was spring! When spring arrived, so did the bears and Anne's bird feeders were taken down. What was most unusual was being by myself most of the day. There was nobody around either. It was just me, the four leggeds and Tony's presence until Anne returned from work.

I had resumed meditating often before I went to bed. The small sandaled feet came rushing towards me and reached for my hand. We walked quickly down a long, pristine, white hall and reached a door. She opened it. What I saw was totally unfamiliar. It was a landscape with pink grass! The minute I stepped on it the grass turned bright green. It was so bright it made me smile. There was a huge tree some distance from me and I began to realize I was standing on a cliff. I was dressed differently. I had on a white dress that went down to my ankles. Nothing fancy but I remember it being a perfect fit and I looked slightly different, same face but my eyes were jet black and larger. My hair had returned to its original blue-black color, but it was wavy, thicker, falling just above my shoulders. I turned around and Tony was standing there with a satisfied smile. He extended his hand and we walked to that tree I had seen. He let me know that this was our tree. It was thick with branches and leaves unlike anything I'd ever seen. The colors were rich and I could feel the life in this tree. We sat under it and for a few seconds I felt its heartbeat, its life force. There was a benevolence about it that was palpable. Tony put his arm around me and we leaned back against the trunk of our tree. We were twenty feet or so from the edge of the cliff. Sitting there I could see what was at the bottom, a beach with cream colored sand and turquoise water that extended to the horizon where it met a pale pink sky. I was captivated by all of it and wanted to walk on the beach. Instantly, Tony and I were there. I told him that this was wonderful, the colors, the water, the unusual peacefulness of it all yet it exuded a vibrancy and healthiness I had never encountered. A huge sailboat appeared and I wanted to wade in the water and get on the boat. My reservations about boats and water had vanished. I took a few steps towards the water and Tony pulled me back.

"You can't," Tony said. "You can't go in the water."

I turned, looked at him and asked, "Why not?"

Pulling me further back from the water, he said, "When it's time, I'll take you to the other side in our boat."

I was dejected. "The other side...I understand. Do you know when that will be?"

"Not for awhile," he said.

Somehow, we were back on top of the cliff and started walking. He looked at me and said, "You've got to go. You can't stay any longer." Tony nodded his head towards the direction I had arrived, but there was no door, just wide open green land that seemed to be endless. We walked for the equivalent of a city block and the door appeared. It opened and there she was extending her hand.

"Stop worrying. You can come back whenever you want. I've left my body but I will never leave you. Now go." Tony said.

I stepped through the door, took her hand and went back. When I brought myself out of the meditation, I leaned back, exhaled, checked on Amber who was sound asleep next to me, and went to bed. These visits to sit under our tree and gaze out at this strange body of water that was at the bottom of the cliff occurred many times. And the woman who always came for me, whose face I could never clearly see, who was so familiar yet so different fascinated me. I wanted to know who she was so I finally asked. The answer? She's the Eternal You.

Tony's presence on my floor grew stronger and light bulbs started to burn out in rapid fashion. One Friday night I was reading in bed. It was a little after one AM when a voice came through the bugler alarm that was in my living room. It was startling, but I knew no one was breaking in. The voice was scratchy so I couldn't understand anything that was being said. It sounded like a human voice, maybe female, but I couldn't be sure because of the static or whatever the interference was. I sat in bed, unable to move. The voice continued for at least five minutes and then abruptly stopped. I sat in bed for another five minutes, slowly reached to turn out my bedside lamp, and went to sleep.

As I came up the steps the next morning, Anne was in the kitchen.

"You should call someone about the alarm. It went off last night. Some strange voice came through. Maybe it picked up a police scanner. Something's probably wrong with the wiring."

Anne turned and looked at me. "The alarm hasn't worked in two years. I had it disconnected."

The mountains gave me the spiritual security to return to art. I continued to explore abstract pastels. Right after Tony died, I started doing these and stopped after I sold the country place. Now I could get back to them. I set up a little corner in what Anne called her sunroom and started. I had several sets of soft pastels. I opened all of them, selected some paper and began. I'd line everything up as best I could in such as small space. Surgical gloves went on next, and then I waited for one of the colors to call me. I found my hands still reaching for shades of blue. Anne walked in one day, looked at the work and said, "You know, you've done a lot with blue."

I looked up at her and thought about Lucinda's reaction to the work I had started right after Tony died. "Yeah... I'm just drawn to that color. It probably has something to do with Tony." She looked at the pastels, then looked at me and walked away. I was on creating a body of "blue works" all for Tony. I churned them out for quite awhile. Eventually some of the larger works became part of a two woman show in one of the local gallery areas in a nearby town.

It was early Spring of 2012 when I received a call from Jared Kirkland. Jared's Dad, Dr. Charles Kirkland, was not only my first doctor after leaving my Pediatrician's care, he was the closest thing I had to a father while growing up in New York. Thankfully the Kirkland family lived two blocks from us in Riverdale. I spent a lot of time at their house, sometimes weeks, when things got too crazy in my house. They were my second family, Jared and his sisters, Kristen and Alexandra. Their mother, Julia, was also a medical doctor, a hematologist. She was responsible for my love of cooking and introducing me to Zabar's as a teenager. Somebody in the Kirkland family was related to the founders.

Julia died back in the seventies from cancer. In many ways, she was my first personal loss. I was devastated when she passed. The last time we saw each other she was in bed at home. That's where she wanted to die. She made me promise that I wouldn't end up sleeping alone, and asked me to "please, take care of Kristen. Watch over her."

Now thirty plus years later, her son was calling to tell me his father died. He had been ill for some time, spending the last year of his life on a ventilator. The news wasn't a surprise but I still felt like I was sucker punched and told Jared that I couldn't talk. I hung up knowing that when Dr. Kirkland was buried, volumes of my life would go with him, and I was going to feel a little less safe in the world.

So many people who were important to me, so many friends had died, I began to wonder why I was left standing, and not in New York but in northern New Hampshire with a view of Mt. Washington, living in a village that was smaller in population than the high school I attended! There had to be a reason.

CHAPTER EIGHTEEN

Visits & Signs

The air of northern New Hampshire and the location of this small village created something like a "perfect storm" of psychic possibilities. It had something to do with ley lines, New England's geometric arrangement of sites going back to great antiquity, the height of the mountains, and the record of anecdotal extraordinary experiences. Without any strategic effort on the part of the Mount Washington Valley's Chamber of Commerce the area embraces a range of alternative practitioners, psychics, healers, mediums, animal whisperers, and naturopathic doctors. I ended up in the right place for all that was about to finally blossom.

Meditating was never difficult for me, but here it became extraordinary. I had developed a habit of asking a question before starting. After experiencing a glimpse of my wedding that happened in some other time line or dimension, I was curious about what else I could access regarding the life I almost had with Tony. Ask and ye shall receive? I did.

The first five to seven minutes of centering myself eventually gave way to a residential scene. It was a house somewhere in an urban area that I vaguely remembered but couldn't identify. Tony and I had just moved in and opened boxes were everywhere. He had on jeans and a white shirt, and looked slightly aggravated and tired. For some reason I had on a skirt, a pale blue shirt and had kicked off my shoes. I was sitting on the floor and heard myself say, "Take a break. Sit down," and I motioned to the space next to me. "I'll get you something to drink," I said to Tony.

"No, I'm okay." He sat down right next to me and put his arm around my shoulders. We looked at each other and smiled, content and relieved that we had finally found a house. One kiss led to another and another. We were way beyond kissing when someone knocked on the front door.

Tony groaned and put his shirt on. I ran upstairs to our bedroom, half dressed, where I changed into a pair of jeans and another shirt. When I came back down, I found Tony talking to our new neighbors who lived next door. Then it all faded.

I was shocked by the clarity of what I saw, the colors, the layout, the furniture and what we looked like, a little different but the same. Tony was a slimmer but still very fit. I was a taller by two or three inches. His hair was the same, with that wonderful gradation from black to grey. Mine? Still short, unruly, jet-black, and very thick, waves and curls, but straight. We were both the exact same color, a peculiar red-beige. Our eyes were black. It made me think we were from the same tribe. Society was organized differently here.

I could return to this scene whenever I wanted to and see it replay like a movie. There were additional scenes regarding this life. Public transportation ran on some kind of electromagnetic energy reducing the noise we associate with buses and subways.

Individual cars were few. I saw our dining room, part of our kitchen, the front hall, a media room, his office, our bedroom. There was a scene revealing the birth of our first child, a son we named Zachary, the maternity ward that had a futuristic element, a Thanksgiving dinner, what we did for work, a second home near the water where I saw our daughter who was two or three months old curled up on Tony's chest sound asleep, and one scene at a cemetery. In this timeline, I died first. I was an architect and a crane fell on me at a construction site. Several of my internal organs were crushed. I lived long enough for Zachary to arrive at the hospital from graduate school where he was studying architecture. This was the son who graduated from Yale. Tony and our children were with me when I died. There was a graveside service on a cloudy day.

These scenes and others were so vivid and "real" I could smell the ocean air in one, feel the summer heat in another, and hear our children playing. I was so grateful for these scenes but they also refueled a need to talk to Tony in the here and now. I wanted him to come back, to sit next to me in this dimension, and tell me what this was about! There was so much left unsaid, undone. What has he learned on the other side about himself, about me?

I knew he heard me. One night I saw him briefly standing at the foot of my bed looking frustrated as I fell asleep. Seeing through the veil to the other side had its limitations. The truth was I didn't know what I was looking for short of him coming back or me going there. At the very least I needed to talk with him, in this dimension or something pretty close to it. Some people would say I needed a miracle or a very good shrink specializing in grief therapy.

Christine said when I shared some of this with her, "Janis, that's impossible. Are you okay? The mountain air is kinda thin up there. You sure it hasn't affected your brain?"

I laughed and said, "Not at all. My brain is fine. No tumors. No disease, okay? I can't be the only one who's gone through this. Somebody's got to know something."

I remember Christine screeching, "*Know what?* Look, you've got to let this go. Just let it go."

"I can't," I said. "I don't know what's driving this, but I can't let it go. Something is happening."

"Why isn't it enough to talk to him in your mind, you know? Just have a chat. You said you could do that."

"It's not enough because it just isn't, Christine." I paused for a minute then asked, "Why is this upsetting *you*?"

Christine was quiet. I waited and then she said, "Because it's impossible, Janis. All of it. I mean, I believe *you*. Believe what *you've* told me because it's *you*, but ..."

"But what?" I asked.

"It frightens me, Janis. I don't understand it. It defies everything I know. Defies science, logic." Christine said.

"What if science doesn't have all the answers? What if science is in denial? There's a lot of information out there that people are refusing to look at. Scientific information, my friend."

Christine said nothing.

"Look, I know you grew up in the church. When you went to Sunday School and the subject was Easter...resurrection, etc., did you think it was a fairy tale? Forget the bunnies and the dyed eggs. What do you tell your kids? How do you deal with Easter now?" I asked.

"I don't deal with it," she said. "I can't!"

"Why?"

"Why? Because I don't know how to hold the impossible, okay? I'm going to leave that to you."

"I'm beginning to think the impossible is anything beyond our understanding. If we can't understand it, nor conceive of it, we dismiss it as being foolish or crazy or worse say it can't exist."

Christine muttered, "Well maybe. Maybe it can't."

"Maybe nothing," I said! "C'mon Christine. Think about it. If someone told our great-great grandparents that one day we would be able to do heart transplants or go to the moon, or use a plastic card to get money from a machine, they would've thought the person was either crazy or possessed."

"Have you read the papers lately? Who's to say we aren't crazy or possessed? Look, I just can't deal. That's all I'm saying. I can hardly handle this life, never mind the afterlife or anything in between!"

I laughed and changed the subject. I knew Christine well. I could tell she was on the verge of flipping out. I retreated. After our conversation, I pulled out some notes I had taken on afterlife research. There seemed to be a lot of people in the United Kingdom who had explored this subject. There was a Nobel Prize winner, Sir Joseph Thompson, who looked into this phenomenon. (He had discovered the electron.) There was a Dr. Richet from the Sorbonne who collaborated with another Nobel Prize winner and came up with the term ectoplasm. I was fascinated by this substance. Under the right conditions, some physical mediums can produce excessive amounts of ectoplasm. It appears to act as a conduit through which those on the other side can manifest for a short amount of time. Dr. Richet conducted an experiment before 150 people where the ectoplasm came through as *sparkling little flecks*. Other records indicate that those who've passed over came back whole body and soul, if only for a short amount of time.

I kept digging for more information and found an organization here in the U.S. called The Afterlife Research Institute., another one called The Silver Cord. I was continually amazed at how much was out there if you looked. I'd sit up and read and read, trying to understand what's been discovered. What are the theories? What's actually happened? What does it mean to die? What are those last moments like? What about the reality of eternity? What about time? Why are we so afraid? What can we learn from near-death experiences and verified cases of reincarnation? It's all out there. But this phenomenon of ectoplasm, physical mediums? So much of what I read took place in the United Kingdom. The U.S. seems to be playing "catch-up."

Whenever I'd be reading or researching this, it was clear to me I wasn't alone. It wasn't just Tony who was around, but there were others. I didn't recognize them at first, but in time I was told after I asked that they were teachers, guides and even one former colleague from the other side who were looking over my shoulder reading along with me.

Desperate for verification of what I was experiencing, I asked the gallery owner where my work was being shown if she knew of any good psychics in the area. She did and gave me the name and number of a psychic medium saying this person was *very* good. I called and made an appointment. I needed somebody to tell me something or at least verify what I was going through!

At the appointed day and time, I drove over to see her and I couldn't find her office. I drove up and down a winding road where her office was supposed to be three times, and saw nothing! I returned to the house, called her associate and told her I couldn't find the place and asked for clearer instructions. This was one of those times when I longed for Manhattan's grid system, where streets crossed avenues, and Fifth Avenue separated east from west. I also told her I wanted the next earliest opening. They had a cancellation that opened up right before I called that I could have.

"Great," I said. "I'll take it. What's the date?"

It was my birthday. I laughed and said, "Of course."

The next time I found where her office was located. I parked my car in a make-shift parking lot next to the house, and walked in after looking at the wooded area behind the house. I sighed and thought, this is one very "crowded" area, referring to the spirit life especially of Native Americans still wandering the grounds. There was a very heavy feeling inside the house that had been converted into offices and meeting spaces. I didn't like it. The atmosphere made me uneasy. I sat in the waiting room for a few minutes noting that the wood paneling didn't help lighten the feeling of gloom. I believe that houses and land hold the energy of all inhabitants who have lived there. In this house there were too many people with unresolved issues that you couldn't see but feel. This was one of those structures that was always dark regardless of the weather, just like the dining room in our house down south. The feeling wasn't sinister or threatening but it wasn't welcoming or comfortable either. Whatever went on there I wanted nothing to do with it. I shifted my weight in the chair and continued to wait.

A tall, beautiful, blonde haired woman walked in to greet me. She introduced herself. I was stunned. I didn't know what a psychic medium should look like, but this one could've been a Vogue model! We went upstairs to her office that was renovated attic space. I sat down opposite of her and said, "Look, I'm not here to find out how to win the lottery! I'm just looking for some information to help increase my understanding." That's all I said.

I thought I would see just how good this woman was. I was giving her absolutely nothing!

She leaned back, crossed her long legs and nodded her head. Then she explained how she worked. She was "just a channel for whom ever came through." She would first tell me some information about how they died and that would help me identify them. The session would be recorded and emailed to me shortly afterwards.

She took a deep breath, let it out and I waited but not for very long. She described a man who stepped forward. She sensed a lot of water in his lungs and said he drowned in a large body of water. That got my attention.

"He's saying that he had no idea who you really were and he apologizes for leaving so soon. He has a bouquet of white roses that he's laying at your feet. And he's standing right behind you now and wants you to know... He's saying, 'I may have left my body but I will never leave you.' She looked at me and said, "You're going to get a bouquet of white roses soon. You will."

She was doing fine until then. I didn't think there was a decent florist between here and Portland, Maine. I could be a terrible snob. Where would these roses come from?!

She went on and took time to explain Tony's statement about not knowing who I really was in terms of my soul identity.

"Had he only known," she said. "Over there, you see each other's soul. The physical body?" She motioned with her hand to indicate that it was of little to no importance in the afterlife.

During our session, she also conveyed messages from Kae and Dr. Kirkland. She told me that whenever I saw a bear or bears, Dr. Kirkland was trying to get my attention. I laughed. The day before I came to see her, three bears walked through our backyard. She looked right at me when I told her and said, "See! Anytime you see them…" She wasn't wrong. The Kirkland "kids" who were now adults followed their family tradition of vacationing in New Hampshire. When I drove down to Moultonboro to see them the following year, I saw a bear cub out of the corner of my eye run across a side road. I had read somewhere that the people who come through during a reading with a Medium were often the people you had the closest relationships with in this dimension. That's exactly what happened. Kae told me that she was so glad I had gotten out of my own way and landed here. She was so proud of me for doing that.

I left the Medium's office amazed, and drove back to the house thinking about everything that had come through her to me. But those white roses…not so much I thought. Nobody's perfect. When I got back I went online to check my facebook page.

"Anne," I shouted. "Can you come here?"

She walked in the living room and asked, "What is it?"

I pointed to the facebook page and said, "Tell me what you see?" I'm sure she thought I was crazy.

She looked at the page and then looked at me. "Roses. White roses."

"You do see white roses, yes? Against a maroon background? That's what you see?"

"Yes," she said, puzzled and looked at me. "White roses on a maroon background."

"Okay, now tell me who or where it's from? You know posts indicate where or who they're from at the top on the left. Tell me, if you see the instructions at the bottom...you know, 'Like, Comment, Share.' Do you see all that?"

She looked back at the post and I saw her face go still. "Oh..."

"It's not there is it? So how did this post get there?" I asked. "Looks like someone just slapped it up there."

Anne was baffled. I told her what the Medium said. Things changed dramatically for me after that reading.

CHAPTER NINETEEN

Reality Broadens

Over time, the Medium and her associate, who was a Reiki practitioner, and I became friends, not that we hung out, because I couldn't keep up with these women! I was an advocate and a supporter for both of them. Tony's ongoing presence fit in very nicely with their frame of reference along with a broader community of like minded people. I was still stunned to find this in northern New Hampshire.

Big changes started when I took a seven week psychic development course given by the Medium. I had to come face to face with the reality and/or scope of being a Caulbearer. For some reason I still had doubts because I didn't know where to put these abilities in the context of my life. When I did it was rarely for "the greater good." It was rarely overt unless someone's life was in danger and even then there was always the question, "Well, how do you know this?" The nine-eleven experience made a big impression on me. One of the things Galen told me still stood at the forefront of my mind. "You're not going to give readings. Your gift will be used for something far more subtle with a profound impact." Perhaps some of this would be revealed in this course.

Over a dozen people had signed up. We sat in a large semi-circle while the Medium talked. I was fine until we had a specific class on psychic readings. It was the Medium's belief that *everyone* is capable of doing this. We had to learn how to tap into those undeveloped areas of our brain; ninety percent of our brain is dormant, unused and rarely thought about. That made perfect sense to me, but... the exercise was simple. Two of us would be called upon to come to the front of the room, sit opposite of each other, hold hands, and tell what information or insights we picked up about the other. Seated on the far right of the semi-circle, I felt like I was in high school, praying that the teacher wouldn't call on me! Not only was I "unprepared" I knew I was unable to do a reading. I mean, c'mon! I kept hoping I would vanish or someone else would be called upon. Maybe the Medium and her associate would forget I was there. The Medium called on an older woman. Thank-God I thought. And then she called on me.

I begged off. "No, I really can't do this," I said.

She looked at me and said, "Don't you b.s. me, Janis Pryor. Get up here!"

Time to look like a fool, I thought. We were instructed to simply state what comes to us. I silently groaned. As I walked towards this older woman to take my seat across from her a rush of information hit me. I felt like I was walking against the wind. There was a sense of urgency to tell this woman what I was receiving even though the information didn't make itself clear until I actually sat down and took her hand. Then I knew I had to hurry up and tell this woman before the information was taken away by this rush of wind. (Is this the reason so many mediums and psychics talk so rapidly?) I had never met this older woman, never seen her in town. I had no clue who she was.

I sat down and it was as if someone said, "Go!"

With her hands in mine I said, "Standing behind your left shoulder is a little old lady and she's pointing her finger at you, berating you. She's given you a hard time in life and you're still dealing with it. Whatever it is she did, it's scarred you. You've been hurt and it's made your life more difficult. You're still dealing with it." (Maybe it's her mother or someone like that, I thought) I went on for another minute or two and then stopped. Whatever the source of this information or wherever it came from, it was gone. I let go of her hands and had no clue if any of what I said meant anything. I was ready to be outed as a fool or worse, and looked forward to telling the Medium, "See? Told ya' I couldn't do this."

The woman sighed and smiled at me. The Medium, who was standing behind me, looked at the woman and asked, "Did this make any sense?"

"Oh yes," she said.

"And what did I tell you a few days ago when you came to see me?"

"Almost the exact same thing."

"Okay – tell her," the Medium instructed the woman.

"You saw my mother. And she did make my life very difficult."

I was shocked. "My God, this is real," I thought. Didn't all mothers and daughters have some conflicts? Of course they did. But this was *a little old lady shaking her finger*, that's what distinguished what I said. That was the identifying phrase along with stating that she had been *terribly scarred and it continued to impact her life.*

It was never like I hadn't sensed this kind of personal information about other people. I had but I would keep it to myself. All I had to do was focus and concentrate but it was the shock of having it confirmed by someone else.

I didn't have to hold their hands but culling this information was often uneven but it was representative of the information I could pick up without too much effort. It didn't happen with everyone unless they played a role in my life for better or worse or unless I was "ambushed" by being in a crowd of people. It was a rush of information, too many sensations and images, so I stayed away from events that had large crowds. Sitting in church was often like scanning emotional x-rays with psychic footnotes. Going to a party was torture for me so I rarely went out.

Work was a different matter. Sitting in a meeting, working in a campaign, interviewing a guest, I felt like I was working in a lab. I had an interesting skill. What was much more consistent was *detecting someone's true intent and what motivated them.* But what happened in the Medium's class was a whole other thing. The immediacy of the confirmation, the specificity that elevated it from the general to the specific, I had to accept the scope of these abilities.

Then I had to be "read." She talked about being in leadership positons and working with leaders. But the one thing that the other woman said stood out.

She asked, "You know anybody who's name starts with the letter 'F'?"

I shook my head. "No, can't think of anyone," I said.

"Well, he's here and he's asking for forgiveness. He says he's really sorry for what he did to you."

Then I knew what the 'F' stood for, father. It was my father who came through. The best I could do was let everything go that he and Tina had done to me. I was fascinated that *he* asked for forgiveness. It meant he understood the damage he did. Tina never understood and never came through any reading I had.

When the course concluded four things happened that were significant from my point of view. One of the classes addressed automatic writing. *We had to try*. The class went into a meditative state where the Medium called in the Angels. Then we were supposed to just write what came through. I did this with my eyes closed. That helped me concentrate. It was like opening the flood gates! I wrote and wrote and wrote the first time we tried. When we were brought out of our meditative state, I looked down at my note pad. My eyes widened and I frowned. I could barely read what I wrote! I looked around to see if anyone else showed any signs of confusion or bafflement. There were quite a few looking stunned and confused. I also noticed that the Medium's mother had been watching me.

The Medium told us, "If your writing looks like chicken-scratch, don't worry. Angels don't have a need to write!" I laughed. It was true. Why would an angel have to write? This is why I could barely read what *they* had written through me. *I* wasn't writing it! I learned to go over each page I'd written immediately after I stopped. Eventually, as I was re-writing the entries into a legible script after a session additional information would come. Often, they – the Angels or other entities – would stay to make sure I got it right. I knew this information wasn't coming from some forgotten room in my unconscious. I knew what it was like to write from a stream of consciousness. This was different; the language, the phraseology, the guidance. After the classes, my Angel sessions continued taking place in my bedroom usually after midnight.

The energy in my bedroom gradually changed and I believe something in me shifted also. This change was indicated by an extraordinary series of nosebleeds over three to four months. I was accustomed to severe nosebleeds. They started at the age of five. The usual treatment was cauterization, sealing off the ruptured vessel by burning it shut. I got used this. It was another feature of my childhood.

Now, they were infrequent, so when they started again I was surprised. These nosebleeds had me waking up in the morning, choking on my own blood. It poured from my left nostril. It was often thirty to forty minutes before I was able to stop the bleeding. As the days went by I began to feel weak. One morning when I pulled out what looked like a seven to eight inch rope of blood from my left nostril, I knew it was time to go to the hospital. A specialist was called in because after the first cauterization, the bleeding didn't stop. My nose was cauterized on four separate occasions over four months. The last cauterization left the bridge of my nose so tender and sore, it hurt to wear glasses. Had the nosebleeds not stopped, the specialist was considering some kind of procedure that required anesthesia. He finally admitted after my last visit that he had become "a little concerned." The Medium said my system was being purged.

If Tony was around during this time, I didn't sense it, but I continued to talk to him, still angry that he had left too soon. I worked hard at staying in touch with his sister, Cathy. There were many times when I wanted to give up, just let it go. When calls weren't returned, I believed she really didn't like me. In five minutes or less I had myself believing all sorts of things, none of them good. The few times I did manage to reach her on the phone, it just "happened." I remember once as I sat down on the couch to read and watch television something said, "call her now." I did and reached her. This happened four times and during one of those calls I told her about the Medium. I wanted Cathy to come up and have a reading with her. The Medium did have phone clients but there was something to be said for sitting in the room with her. It took three years to get Cathy up here. She and her new husband arrived one Saturday. He was a sweet, gentle man completely lost when it came to helping Cathy deal with her grief.

Meanwhile, I told Cathy about writing this book. The first version was "based on true events..." It allowed me to address some other issues that hounded Tony's life and my life. I felt strongly about them but the truth has its own power. I remember the look on Cathy's face when I told her. I knew how surprised she would be. I tried to tell her about some of Tony's "visits," but she couldn't hear it. She had no room for it in her head, heart or soul. I knew there were days when all she could do was breathe from one moment to the next.

The third change happened in my bedroom regarding an amaryllis plant. The first year I was in northern New Hampshire some friends came to visit and gave me this amaryllis plant. I loved it! Usually, an amaryllis blooms once and then they're dormant. Most people throw them away after the first blossoms. I didn't. I kept this one, put it on my dresser, and all but forgot about it for two years! Shortly after the nose bleeds stopped, I noticed the amaryllis was growing. A green shoot started to rise from the bulb. I expected it would grow several inches and die. It didn't. The bulb produced four flowers on two stalks. That would've been enough for me but it didn't stop. The flowers were over six inches wide. The stalks were just under twenty inches. Their growth felt magical! Anne was spooked by them. She wanted to know what was I doing? I looked at her and said,

"Nothing. I don't know what's going on." Cathy told me that Tony had "a way" with plants.

By this time, Anne no longer thought I was a little crazy and considered living with me was an adventure. There was a one two punch that nailed the fourth change. It began with another episode of the disconnected burglar alarm talking again, the same scratchy, unintelligible voice. Only this time Anne heard it, and came flying down the stairs. I chuckled as she ran into my living area. "That's what I'm talking about," I said. "This is what happened the last time."

Weeks later we were watching television when we heard a strange ringing sound similar to a telephone. It wasn't coming from the extension in the living room and it wasn't coming from our cell phones.

"What is that?" I asked. "It sorta sounds like the phone but it's different." The ringing continued.

"Where's it coming from?" Anne asked.

I stood up. "Let's follow the noise." I walked over to the stairs and realized it was coming from my level. Maybe it was the disconnected alarm!

Anne and I slowly went down the stairs. When we got there we realized the sound was coming from my bedroom. We walked in and the ringing was coming from the extension that was on my bedside table. No other extensions in the house made a sound. It was a moment neither one of us will forget. We stood there frozen in place, looking at it until it stopped. I don't know why one of us didn't answer it. This was one of those times when I wished I drank! Wide eyed, Anne looked at me. I stood there staring at the phone and then I looked around my bedroom with no idea what I was looking for. I walked back upstairs and thought to myself, "You've done it now." In my gut, I knew that by not answering that phone, I had pushed the envelope. I just didn't know how far, but I sensed I would find out.

CHAPTER TWENTY

Some Information

I slowly gained more insight about the selection of the Emissary.

A year after Tony instructed me to write this, I wanted to visit his grave on his birthday and place some flowers on the gravesite because that's what one did! I felt guilty for being so lax especially in light of his sister's constant visits. I knew she was closer but still… I knew I needed to do this.

Amber and I made the long drive down, purchased some white roses, and headed to the cemetery. I thought I remembered the exact location of his grave site. I didn't and got lost. The cemetery was divided in two beautifully landscaped sections that were mirror images of each other. I didn't notice that on my previous visit. I hate being lost. After making several wrong turns, I asked for instructions from one of the workers. I eventually found Tony's grave.

I was angry and frustrated and vented to Tony about getting lost. I heard him say, *"You know, you don't have to come here to find me!"* It's what I'm supposed to do, I told him. I heard him quietly laugh and saw him shake his head from side to side. That pissed me off more! I stood at his grave fuming. When I got back in the car I could barely see straight. Amber got in the back seat as I slowly drove out of the cemetery and that's when the Emissary's face popped up in front of me for just two or three seconds, and I smiled. "Here's hoping that at least he's having a good birthday, that he's with friends and family who care for him." It gave me enormous comfort to consider that and I calmed down.

As I drove back, I chuckled recalling how Tony eventually showed me exactly why he chose this man to be his Emissary. The fact that they had so much in common was enough for me, but it wasn't everything. The Emissary continued to enjoy a great deal of popularity due to the ongoing success of his television series. Along with millions of other viewers I got hooked. Once a week, no one was allowed to call, to interrupt, nothing. Anne thought I was crazy and fled to her bedroom when the show came on. At the appointed time, I sat on the couch with Amber next to me, and lost myself in this show for an hour each week. I was puzzled by the depth of my reaction to this show. I'd find myself close to tears or weeping silently while watching some scenes between the two lead characters.

One week there was an intense romantic scene between the Emissary and his female lead. Women across America melted. While watching this scene, out of the corner of my eye a flicker of light caught my attention. I turned and looked. Seated in one of my club chairs was Tony. His leg was crossed. He wore a pair of khaki Bermuda shorts, a blue shirt, and the most remarkable, seductive grin I've ever seen. He tilted his head towards the television and I heard, "See, that's how I feel about you. That's why he was chosen."

"My God," I thought. It made my ears turn red! "What an incredible set of coincidences. The timing was perfect," referring to the show, Tony's death, and the Emissary.

Then I heard Tony say, "There're no coincidences. You know that."

I smiled. He was right. What I didn't anticipate was having any connection to the emissary other than being a fan and enjoying the similarities between him and Tony. He was Tony's person, not mine! One day while puttering around the house, I heard, "*You've got to contact him,*" and it wasn't Tony's voice.

"Why?" I asked and what I saw was the word *loss* and heard, "*You have to do it by the end of the year.*" It was early December. He was going to lose someone important to him. What was I supposed to do? I would have an easier time getting through to the White House than contacting this man and what would I say? *You would tell him that life is everlasting and not to worry.* A month later the emissary's father died.

Tony's ethereal appearances, sensing him when I couldn't see him, and light bulbs being constantly replaced on my level became routine. But this need I had for something more continued to eat away at me. It wouldn't go away. I had some additional readings with the Medium where Tony came through. It wasn't enough.

He wanted me to be happy, to enjoy this life. I had no idea how I was going to do that, all things considered. He was also very busy on the other side, engaged in "remarkable things" that could impact us in this dimension.

"I can hardly wait to show you everything," he said in one reading.

That can't happen too soon, I thought to myself. Life on this side had some definite drawbacks. What I referred to as "the Earth thing" wasn't working too well for scores of people, not to mention the planet and it's inhabitants.

How many times have I heard that the earth is a school where we're sent to learn. While I loved to learn and read, I had never been fond of school. There were long stretches of near fatal boredom during high school. Earth was not boring but injustice was everywhere, ugly, obvious and deadly. We kept making the same mistakes over and over. I hated repetition as much as I hated boredom. The older I got, the more I wondered why I was here at all. As Kae often said to me, "There's got to be a better place."

Three books gave me comfort. In addition to *Keep Going*, there's *The Invitation*, by Oriah Mountain Dreamer and *Anan Cara* by John Donohue. These books shored up my beliefs in the power of truth, the necessity of justice, the eternity of wisdom, and the moral duty to respect love. There was a line in *The Invitation* that deeply resonated with me. "I want to know what sustains you from the inside, when all else falls away..." What sustained me when all else fell away was God's breath. That was easy. What wasn't easy to accept was that, "...knowledge will never be enough..." What we need is, "the wisdom to live with what we do not know, what we cannot control, what is painful – and still choose life..."

What we do not know is not the same as what we choose not to know. There was contemporary knowledge on the afterlife, work being done by legitimate doctors and scientists now. It was no longer enough to know what had been done a hundred years ago. I needed to know what was happening *now* because as Old Hawk said in *Keep Going*, "...the journey all of us are making is one of constant learning...without knowledge we cannot achieve wisdom." I needed that knowledge to live with Tony's loss, and find the wisdom within that loss, to prepare myself for something that was coming soon. I couldn't shake that feeling. It's the sensation that makes you look over your shoulder when you know someone or something is watching you.

I reflected on one of the things Galen said when we talked back in Manhattan. She told me that, "From the moment Tony first spoke to you, it was the beginning of a very different life for you." It made me very still.

CHAPTER TWENTY-ONE

...eyes to see and ears to hear...

If you've ever lived in the South, spring is glorious, abundant and lush. It really does start in March and never later than Easter. If you've ever lived in northern New England, spring is often a concept hiding in the muck of mud season. But it does come. This was nature's version of testing your faith if you lived this far north. Geo-politics was completely obvious here. Friends asked me why I stayed in the mountains, more specifically northern New Hampshire, a part of the country not noted for its friendliness to people of color although there were signs of change.

"That may be," I often said. "And I've felt some hostile stares and some shocked expressions from people who looked like they had never seen anyone who wasn't white. There's nothing I can do about that. They need to get out more!" Too many friends, black, white, red and yellow were convinced I would either regain my sanity and return to 'civilization,' to New York where I could walk to Zabar's or I would die a slow intellectual death from lack of stimulation and the absence of haute couture! Sensing my needs, several friends from New York actually made the pilgrimage to the "far north" of New England to see me.

Practically, it was a lot cheaper to live here. I didn't know how long that advantage would be enough to prevent me from leaving. The deciding factor keeping me here, so far, was this troubling feeling that I was supposed to be here. This place gave me the creative space to draw and work with pastels and write. I considered that enough of a gift for me to remain put.

Leaving her children and husband in Manhattan, Christine came up for the weekend twice. She hopped on a bus and took the long ride to visit me. The bus stopped at the covered bridge. I picked her up on Friday and she couldn't get over the surroundings.

"Gurl, there's a covered bridge! And a lot of trees!" I put her things in the back seat of my car and we drove to the house with her commentary all the way. "You've got to be kidding me! This is it?" she asked. "This is downtown? It's only two blocks!"

"Christine, it's a village, okay. Roughly nine hundred people," I said trying not to giggle at her.

"No Starbucks?"

"Gotta drive almost ten miles to Starbucks. But there is a bakery here that makes pretty good coffee according to what I hear. They make great scones too."

"Hmph! Okay," she said and paused for a moment. "Look, I needed to see where you were. And I want to meet this Anne person. Who is she again?"

"Anne is Claire's sister. You remember me telling you about Claire."

"Claire... oh yeah. She was one of your upscale East Side friends," Christine said. As we continued to drive up a winding hill, Christine asked, "Are there *any* Democrats up here?"

I laughed. "Yeah, I found them! You'd be surprised," I said. "Didn't need a secret hand shake or anything!" We talked politics until we got to the house. I gave her a tour and put her suitcase in my office that doubled as a guest room, a reality imposed by a lack of space that I hated. The house was bigger than it looked but not big enough from my perspective. There was no studio space and no space for my dining table that I loved.

After dinner and after Anne went to bed, I knew Christine wanted to ask me about Tony, but I waited for her to bring it up, and she did.

Christine leaned forward in her chair and asked, "Have you let go of Tony? Maybe you needed to get up here to do that. Once that's done, you can come back to civilization. There're no street lights out here!"

I smiled and proceeded to tell her about this new reality I had entered. I knew this was not what she wanted to hear, but I continued. I told her about all the reading I'd been doing, the research on the afterlife and related issues, the Medium and the unexpected community of alternative practitioners. We stayed up until 2 AM talking, reviewing, gossiping, but I could sense Christine's worry and doubt. A few stories about seeing wild turkeys in flight, bears sighted, moose and deer brought her back to the immediacy of now. I got up to take Amber out before going to bed.

"You're going outside?" Christine asked.

"Yeah, why?"

"It's really dark out there," Christine said. "No lights."

"Come out with me. I want to show you something. Put on a sweater."

"I don't know…"

"Christine, c'mon! Let's go," I said.

"Okay," Christine muttered and followed me.

We stood out in the yard and I said, "Christine, look up."

We both looked up while Amber did some quick sniffing before relieving herself. "One of the wonderful things about living here is the unobstructed view you have of the sky. It's magnificent."

"Oh my God… Janis, it feels like you could just jump up and grab a handful of stars. I'm such a city person." Christine stared at the sky, her mouth partly opened and then she jumped a little. "What was that?"

"What was what?" I asked.

"Didn't you hear that? Like who-who-who," Christine said.

"That's what an owl sounds like." Amber was ready to go back inside. I opened the door and she and Christine rushed back to the living room. She turned and looked at me.

"What?" I asked while taking off Amber's leash.

"You feel closer to him up here don't you?"

I paused before saying anything. "Something like that, yes," I said. "He's here often. I see him and I hear him, and that's just the way it is."

When I took Christine back to the bus stop Sunday afternoon, she wanted to know when I was coming down for a visit. I didn't know. It would be hard with Tony gone and Christine living in the same building as he had. The passage of time wasn't making it easier.

I had started staying up very late and into the early hours when stillness was at its best. If I got to bed at 2:30 AM that was an early night. So much time had passed since Tony's death, and I was still searching, still frustrated by Tony's absence from this realm, and my inability to find a reputable physical Medium.

There was so much left unsaid and that fact often brought me close to tears. Maybe I just wanted to have him here, to throw my arms around him or grill him again about taking twenty years to speak to me. I wanted to convince him to go to Santorini, Greece, to make time to finish those political discussions, to talk about that life we never had together because of that damned boat accident that still made no sense to me at all, to walk down Fifth Avenue at Christmas and look at the Cartier building wrapped up in a red bow, to see a show, have a fabulous dinner out, or just feel my hand in his.

I usually sat up reviewing all this in my mind, but on this night I decided to go to bed instead. My grief was a steady drop of water that never let up. Something was missing in me or I was empty in a way I had never known before. I turned out all the lights in the living room and kitchen, checked to see if the windows and front door were locked. I picked up Amber and placed her on the floor. She walked over to the stairs and proceeded down as I turned on the lights for the stairway. I followed her and noticed one of the recessed lights flickering on and off. I thought, not again. I continued walking down the stairs, and as soon as I set foot in my living area, I knew something was off.

Instead of going in the bedroom as she usually did, Amber jumped up on the couch. Although the door to my bedroom was open, all I could see from where I was standing was the nightstand and the pillows leaning against the headboard. I just stood there and felt anxiety gradually invade my body. I took some deep breaths to calm myself. Okay, I said.

The light on my nightstand had been turned on earlier in the evening, but it seemed different. The light was almost silver. Amber looked at me and barked once. This is silly, I thought. Get a grip! I crossed the living room space and walked over to my bedroom. As soon as I got to the door, I froze. Tony was sitting on the foot of the bed. There was nothing ethereal about him. He was in three dimensions. Slightly bent over and leaning on his elbows, he looked up at me and smiled.

I stood there for a few seconds. "Oh my God," I said out loud.

He put his finger to his lips and I heard him say, "You don't want to wake Anne."

I wanted to run in and hug him. Just as I started, he said, "You can't walk through the door."

"Why not?!"

"It doesn't work that way. Your body can't. The rest of you can," he said.

Staring at him, I said, "Do you mean my consciousness or my ethereal body can? What?"

"Both. You can do it. You've done it whenever you meditate."

I knew exactly what he meant. "What if Anne walks down here? What is she going to see? And Amber?"

"She won't wake up. We've got some help and Amber will be fine."

I wanted to ask who? Who's helping? How? But I put those questions aside. Somehow, I knew we didn't have much time. We communicated telepathically and Tony knew what I wanted to ask.

"You're right. We don't have much time and you can't know everything!" He grinned and then said, "You're so persistent! I've been working really hard with those on the other side to make this happen."

I nodded, sat down on the floor and started to center myself. This happened whenever I went into a meditative state. It grounded me and I could leave my body at the doorway. I stood up and realized I was in some other form. I wasn't pure light but I wasn't solid either. I had never paid a lot of attention to my physical self in a meditative state. Tonight was different.

There was no time to be scared, alarmed or hesitant. Looking down, I did have on a dress much like the one I had seen myself in during another meditative journey. Although others would call this an out of body experience, that didn't feel right to me. I wasn't able to fly around and look down on myself but I couldn't worry about that now. All I wanted to do was walk into my bedroom and sit next to Tony. He was finally here.

Tony stretched out his arm towards me and opened his hand. "Now," he said.

I walked right in, put my hand in his and sat next to him on the bed. Neither one of us was solid as in flesh and blood, but the word gelatinous came to mind. We held our form. I touched his face and his skin felt similar to Galen's. I was flooded with a mix of emotions, joy, gleefulness, happiness, fear, curiosity and the overwhelming depth of this miraculous connection.

"Why did you leave? Why did you have to die so soon?" I asked.

He took my hand and said, "I had overstayed my time, but I couldn't, wouldn't leave without us happening. Nothing was going to stop us. Nothing was going to stop our love. You were my purpose for being in this life time. Our souls agreed to this. But I had to go. If I'd stayed any longer you couldn't do what you have to do now. Remember what I told you, tell our story. People need to know. Our partnership is based on that and this love we have. We should've had a lifetime. Deep down you know that but *it's not your time to leave.* If it's any comfort to you, you can see us in other dimensions, other timelines. You've already done that."

"Twenty years, Tony. Really?"

"You're never going to forgive me for that are you?" he asked.

"No. Do you realize we could've had a life together? Maybe we would've driven each other crazy but it would've been worth the opportunity to know that! And the emissary? I do understand why you chose him but what am I supposed to do with that? What happens when the series ends?"

"You would think of that!" Tony paused. *"He* needs to meet *you,"* Tony said.

"The Medium said that."

"She's right."

"Why am I *here?* In this part of the country? I know there's a reason."

"I want you to be safe. You're safe here, safer than you'd be in any big city."

"It's going to be bad isn't it?" I asked. "We're all in trouble, aren't we?"

Tony nodded his head. "Listen to me. I'm running out of time. I can't hold this form much longer. I've seen so many of your friends. They were there also to meet me because of *you.* Don't you leave here before it's time. When it is time, I'll come get you, I promise but you've still got so much to do here. I love you.

I always have and always will. Now go. I know you don't want to but there's so much in store for you. It won't be long."

I stood up and looked at him. He smiled and said, "I've been watching you..."

I laughed. "I know," I said not wanting to let go of his hand.

"I'm glad I could make you laugh."

"What if I hugged you?" I asked.

"It won't feel the same just like our hands don't feel the same." He stood up, steadied himself as if he were on a boat and said, "Stop stalling."

I let go of his hand, backed back from him and walked through the doorway. I stepped back in my physical body that was still on the floor cross-legged, looked up, and Tony was gone. The silver glow had also left.

My body felt heavy. It was a tight fit, a size too small for the other me. I held my head in my hands and had to think about what it took to stand up. Ten to fifteen minutes passed before I felt able to stand. It was almost 3 AM. I walked over to Amber, picked her up and put her in my bed. Even though it was very late, I took a shower hoping the steady flow of hot water would help me process what just happened.

By the time I finished showering, washing my face and brushing my teeth it was 3:30 AM. I got in bed still overwhelmed and drained from what happened. I slid down, pulled up the covers, and turned out the light. The room began to fill with the mild fragrance of roses. Lying on my side I felt Amber get up and move down next to my legs. I turned over and was nose to nose with Tony all aglow in a soft yellow light.

"Hey," he whispered.

"I can't believe what just happened," I said. "I know it did, but how do I tell this? Who would believe this?"

"Those who have eyes to see and ears to hear will know. We know. The rest don't matter. They'll eventually find out that life and love are everlasting."

Acknowledgements

It took a village to sustain me while the events and creation of this book unfolded. I'll probably forget some but the individuals below deserve special recognition and a heartfelt thank-you.

For their consistent courtesy, respect and faith in me that lightened the load of my anomalous life and conflicting realities: JP and Cathy of Colonial Drug Store, Nate and Wally at the Sunoco, George at Auto Care Plus in Conway, NH, Arman Manoukian and Alex Abutaleb , Lexus of Watertown.

For becoming my anchor and home in the absence of my grandparents, Trinity Church Boston.

For pushing me back to the world of words, The Reverend David Dill, Priest In Charge, Chapel of Our Savior.

For reminding me that art was in my blood, Linda Trum.

For their generosity, invaluable support, and belief in me: Karin Austin, Lisa Boyd, Dennis Briefer, Jill and Gordon Bertrand, Elizabeth Cook, Dottie Deans, Judith and Doug Fitzsimmons, Jacqueline Granville, Sherry Herman, Gwen and Arthur Klipfel, Lyn May, Professor Peggy McIntosh, Professor Rudy Schild, Geoff Smith, Lydia Spitzer, and Olie Thorp.

For just being there: The Reverend Dr.Wm. Rich, Vicar and Interim Rector, Trinity Church Boston, Joanne Johnson, Marcus Deflorimonte, Toni Phillips, Grace Clark and the late Arville Stephens.

For teaching me that writing well isn't enough, that one must learn how to tell a story, Caryn Stevens, freelance editor.

For the powerful affirmation and confirmation of why I had to write this book and what was going on, Olivia Ducasse.

For demystifying the murky, subjective business of getting published, author coach extraordinaire, Mark Malatesta.

For believing in this book and the others that will follow, Eric and Karen Canton of Canton Literary Management.

For cheering me on and providing feedback, suggestions and comments, "my posse," the Mount Washington Valley Women, Joanne Clarey, Beth Dyer, Anne Garland and Mary F. Power.

For the late Mary Frances Oakley whose spirit permeates everything I do, and for being the first to recognize the importance of "Sailor Man" in my life.

And to my four legged companion, Amber, who was my constant source of joy, strength and determination as I wrote *White Roses*. She witnessed all of it and chose another Cavalier to accompany me on the rest of this journey after she departed.

Last but not least, to Cynthia Uhl, for enduring this process with me, witnessing my transformation and tolerating the mystery and madness of creativity. I do not know how this book would've been written without her computer skills, support and patience.

And to the one who started all of this, Sailor Man, who helped me write this book from the other side.

References

...for the doubters, the skeptics, and those
who want to believe...

- *Answers About the Afterlife: A Private Investigator's 15 Year Research Unlocks the Mysteries After Death,* by Bob Olsen
- *Surviving Death: A Journalist Investigates Evidence for an Afterlife,* by Leslie Kean
- *A Lawyer Presents the Evidence for the Afterlife,* by Victor Zammit and Wendy Zammit
- www.facebook.com/afterlifeevidence, www.victorzammit.com
- *The Risen: Dialogues of Love, Grief & Survival Beyond Death,* by August Goforth & Timothy
- *On Life After Death, revised,* by Elizabeth Kubler-Ross & Caroline Myss
- *Life After Death: The Book of Answers,* by Deepak Chopra
- *Proof of Heaven , Map of Heaven,* both by Dr. Eben Alexander
- *Wolf's Message,* by Suzanne Giesemann
- Afterlife Research & Education Institute, Inc. afterlifeinstitute.org

CPSIA information can be obtained
at www.ICGtesting.com
Printed in the USA
LVHW020421190720
661055LV00013B/1226